Coiled Pottery

Traditional and contemporary ways

BETTY BLANDINO

Coiled Pottery

Traditional and contemporary ways

ADAM & CHARLES BLACK · LONDON

First published 1984 by A & C Black (Publishers) Ltd
35 Bedford Row, London WC1R 4JH

Blandino, Betty
    Coiled pottery.
    1. Coil pottery—History
    I. Title
    738.1   NK3785

ISBN 0-7136-2595-3

Cover photograph: *pot with asymmetrical lip,
oxidised stoneware, 28 cm (1984) by Betty
Blandino*
Facing title page: *Restored Mayan water-pot*

ISBN 0-7136-2595-3

Printed in Great Britain by
BAS Printers Limited, Over Wallop, Stockbridge, Hampshire

Contents

*I dedicate this book to Gwyn for his constant moral
support and generous help, without which it might
never have been finished*

Acknowledgements

Many potters, scholars and institutions helped me generously while I was preparing this book. May I thank them all collectively, and particularly those listed below for help as detailed.

The following potters for information about their work and/or for photographs: Gordon Baldwin, Kenneth R. Beittel, Siddig EL'nigoumi, Ewen Henderson, Michael Hullis, Gabrielle Koch, Elizabeth MacDonald, Magdalene Odundo, Helen Pincombe, Sara Radstone, David Roberts, Mary Rogers, Peter Stoodley, Judy Trim, John Ward, Elsbeth S. Woody, Monica Young.

Keith Nicklin, Keeper of Ethnography, Horniman Museum, for providing me with reprints of a number of his published papers, and photographs, on the potters of Ibibioland, Nigeria.

Anne Woods, Department of Archaeology, University of Leicester, for lending me a number of her research papers – at the time unpublished – on the open firing of ceramics.

John M. Lewis, Department of Archaeology, National Museum of Wales, for directing me towards appropriate material on Medieval pottery.

Vronwy Hankey, for permission to use articles and photographs already published, notably on the potters of Beit Shebab.

Finally, I would like to thank Judith Holden, my editor at A & C Black, for constructive and sympathetic help throughout.

The following institutions for permission to reproduce the photographs, listed by page reference.

Ashmolean Museum: 10, 14 (foot), 28 (right), 36, 67, 74 (top), 76 (top), 77 (top), 106
British Museum: 2, 14 (top), 15, 19 (foot), 62 (right), 64, 70 (foot), 73, 74 (foot), 75, 76 (foot)
Buckinghamshire County Museum: 22, 94
Cleveland County Museum Service: 98
Crafts Council: 55, 87 (foot), 102
Museum of the American Indian, Heye Foundation: 77 (foot), 79
Museum of New Mexico: 30 (main photo), 32, 42, 56–57, 57 (right), 80
National Museum of Wales: 16, 18, 41, 68 (foot), 71 (foot)
Victoria and Albert Museum: 17, 28 (left), 61, 68 (top), 72, 93 (foot)

Crafts magazine: (publication of the Crafts Council) 89, 96
Ceramic Review: 62 (left), 99
Jane Coper: 105 (from *Hans Coper* by Tony Birks)
Photographic and illustrative credits to the following, listed by page reference:

Robert E. Barrett: 87 (top right)
Eric Broadbent: 100 (top)
George Crick: 46 (right)
Wyatt Davis: 30
Tyler Dingee: 32, 42, 56
Angelo C. Garzio (by courtesy of the Editor of *Ceramics Monthly*): 19 (top), 34, 50 (top right), 51 (top middle), 59, 109
Vronwy Hankey: 37, 38 (top left), 50 (left), 58 (top), 82 (top left). Her article, which included several of these photographs appeared first in *Palestine Exploration Quarterly*, 1968, and later in *Ceramic Review*, no. 36, 1975.
Henry Hankey: 83 (line drawing)
Geoffrey Ireland: 24, 35, 45, 58 (foot left), 58 (foot right), 70 (top)
G. O. Jones: 12, 27 (both), 33 (both), 51 (top and foot right), 53 (right)
Jack Leggett: 81 (foot)
Eileen Lewenstein: 62 (left), 99
Christopher Lloyd-Jones: 12–13, 86
Patricia May and Margaret Tuckson: 20 (top), 20 (foot), 29 (foot) 38 (top) 38 (foot), 39 (all); 40; all photographs were taken from their book *The Traditional Pottery of Papua New Guinea* (Bay Books)
Friedbert Meinert: 60
Colin Molyneux: 8
Chris Moyse: 89
Keith Nicklin: 21, 26, 29 (top), 43, 44, 47, 66, 69, 71 (top), 81 (top)
Karen Norquay: 31, 48
Joan Novosel-Beittel: 90
Geoff Onye: 49 (top)
Duncan Ross: 92
Andrew Sanderson: 95
Heini Schneebeli: 23, 88
Lance Smith: 93
David Stein: 80
Jeffrey Tearle: 30 (inset), 46 (top and foot left), 56 (top left), 91 (all),
David Ward: 96
Maria Voyatzoglu: 82, foot (line drawing)
William Wallace: 53 (left)

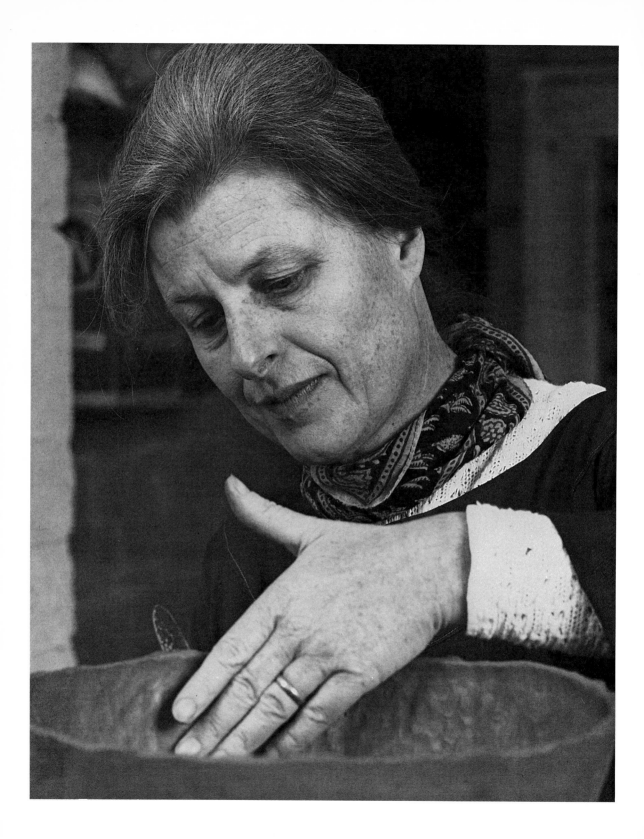

Introduction

This book is about coiling, a way of building pots in which the form grows by the addition of clay in layers, one upon another. They may be as regular as bricks layered to build a wall, as random as dry stone-walling, or as rhythmical as knitting. They may give to the pot the quality of the geological stratification of a cliff face, the wispy structure of a bird's nest, or the organic crumble of the earth's crust – or they may be smoothed to make the surface indistinguishable from that of pots made by other methods.

There are in fact surprisingly few ways of making pots: slabbing, coiling, throwing, casting, moulding and pinching cover most of them. Some are purer than others: for example, a thrown pot is made almost entirely on the wheel; and in casting a pot a particular, limited process is employed. When it comes to coiling it is harder to contain the technique because it spills over into other methods: the clay may be pinched, the coils may be slab-like, the bases may be thrown or moulded. There is a freedom in hand-building which, like most creative processes, can be as inventive, limited, spontaneous, formal, disciplined or careless as the maker chooses.

Coiling and hand-building are often seen as exercises toward 'real' potting – that is, throwing on a wheel. They are, rather, alternative methods – which many contemporary potters have chosen as their means of expression and by which some of the most beautiful pots, from all parts of the world and from many historical times, have been made.

Betty Blandino
Photo: Colin Molyneux (courtesy Welsh Arts Council)

Solid terra-cotta statuette of a naked woman nursing a child, details roughly marked in incisions. Late Cyprus 13th Century B.C.

1

The hand-builders in clay

Given a piece of malleable, soft clay, there are at least two instinctive reactions. One is to pat, squeeze and pull at the lump – arriving at a modelled form like a bird, a man, a head. The other is to beat or roll it into a ball, stick a thumb through the middle and make a crude pot.

To pat, to squeeze, to roll, to dig into, to beat – these are the direct manipulative skills used in hand-forming pots. That first clumsy, holed form can be dragged, squeezed or pinched up; it can be stretched, thinned and formed by beating; it can be patted or slapped into shape. All these methods have been used to make pots – continuous shapes from one piece of clay.

Why coil?

There comes a stage when the clay has been so thinned and shaped that it can no longer be enlarged or grow taller, and yet the form may not be complete. More clay must be added – a coil, a sausage, a strip or a series of pellets of clay.

Now, with the skill to add there is the freedom to build large shapes. It is possible to make very big pots indeed by coiling. In the south of Spain, in Colmenar, wine jars (tinajas) are built 3·5 metres high, with a capacity of 5000 litres. In northern Nigeria a kiln, a granary, or even a house may be built out of thick coils of clay. Coiling can be combined with throwing: in

Thrapsano in Crete, huge pithoi, jars for storing olive oil, are made in this way. Monica Young, who makes large garden pots, 6 feet high, in her Yorkshire studio, says 'it is the only way I know to make large pots'. So coiling is a practical way of building large forms.

But scale is not the only consideration when pots are made by adding clay step by step. It may be imagined that the alternative – pulling a plastic lump of clay into a bowl which is reasonably thin-walled, for instance, is hard to do without a great deal of experience in handling and in choosing the right clay to use. Without that skill and knowledge the pot will sag and flop. By adding clay in stages the speed of working can be adapted continuously to the stiffness or plasticity of the clay; growth can be paced to its condition and to the intricacy of the form. Coiling is a controlled way of building forms.

Most clays are suitable for coiling or hand-building because of this immediacy of control. Neolithic potters had to make use of any clay they could find locally, however gritty or stony. Characteristic ethnic hand-made ware today is also made of local clay which is often very coarse and straight from its source. Such clay might be impossible to refine adequately for throwing, which demands a higher standard of workability based largely on plasticity. Today, the tolerance of hand-building techniques to a variety of clays and plasticity is useful in

Pot by Betty Blandino using coils of a different clay for decorative effect.

experimentation and in the personal, idiosyncratic uses by contemporary potters. Coiling can accommodate the peculiarities of almost any clay mix.

Large controlled forms which may use coarse, open clay or a refined, plastic clay body, or a combination of both, can best be made by coiling. Contemporary potters may exploit other possibilities of this versatile technique, but the virtues they exploit are largely self-confessed aesthetic ones, as we shall see.

The first use of clay

Clay was not first used, as one might have assumed, for utilitarian purposes. It seems that the earliest response to clay was to pinch and model it. Palaeolithic examples of miniature sculptures have been found in many parts of the world – such as the Indus Valley and Mesopotamia.

Monica Young beside her pots.

These small, unfired figures display a freshness and immediacy in the handling of the clay: they may be cult female figures to encourage fertility, men and animals to calm fear and to invoke aid in hunting, or mythical,

magical deities. Meaning and power came through symbol. Herbert Read suggests that prehistoric art was a response to a vital need and that it was 'the first attempt to evade direct causality and influence events from a distance secretly'.*

*from *Icon and Idea* (see Bibliography)

The first pots were made when these nomadic hunters and gatherers settled to farming, keeping animals and cultivating crops. This did not, of course, happen simultaneously all over the world : some of the earliest pottery is found in Anatolia (Turkey) and is attributed to cave-dwelling communities dating from 7000 B.C. ;

13

Neolithic Kansu pot with painted human and animal figures like early cave paintings. 1000–700 B.C.

The thumb and finger prints of Neolithic man used to mark the cigar-shaped mud brick so that it would key to the mortar.

even earlier sherds in the Jōman style (see p. 74) have been found in Japan dating perhaps from 7000 B.C. and continuing until the first Millenium B.C. Pottery did not reach western Europe until about 3000 B.C.

The first small, talismanic idols pre-dated pottery by a few thousand years, and within that time the power of fire to give permanence was found. The magical moment – when it was discovered that the plastic clay would not only dry hard but would also become chemically indestructible once transformed by the red fire – is not known. Yet it is to the permanence of fired clay, and oddly enough to its inherent vulnerability, that we owe much of our knowledge of the life of early man. For though

Neolithic Kansu Yang-shao culture funerary urn, burnished earthenware. 30·5 cm. 2000–1500 B.C.

vulnerable, it does not rust, rot, or easily erode: the objects are still as they were; the thumbprint or the message is as it was made. We share a moment of understanding with a human being hundreds of centuries off.

So clay was first used to make animistic figures: these small objects were magic pieces, believed to be the gods they represented. But the first pots were largely utilitarian, made for the practical necessities of storing, cooking and drinking. Yet because the best – and sometimes the only – examples have been found in burial and ceremonial sites, we know that these too must sometimes have been invested with symbolic significance.

Domestic and funerary ware are not necessarily distinctive, or different. The beautifully decorated Neolithic pots from Kansu Province in China, dating from 2000–1500 B.C.,

are funerary urns. Until recently it had been thought that the variety of scroll patterns on them had a symbolic meaning, but recently pottery has been recovered from habitation sites which has similar patterning.

Almost all the Bronze Age pottery found in Wales has come from burial sites. Again, the relatively small quantity found in settlements does not seem to represent a different ceramic tradition. Shapes which had been developed for domestic purposes were selected and modified for funerary ware, which included beakers, food vessels, cinerary urns and pigmy cups; the interment would be accompanied by elaborate ritual. Of these objects only the pigmy vases, used to hold small bones, or treasures and accessories such as pendants and amulets, were not domestically functional, and it is in these uniquely ceremonial pieces that the greatest variety of shape and pattern occurs.

Bronze Age cinerary urn found in burial mound in Anglesey.

In pre-dynastic Egypt, too, all our knowledge of pottery comes from the tombs, where the dead, arranged in the foetal position, were surrounded by their earthly possessions and provided with food as for a journey – food which was stored in the common pots of the household.

In Cyprus the early settlers are known to us through tombs which were made either out of natural clefts or in chambers cut out of the rock, and contained gifts for the dead, including pottery.

Although the main production of these pots must have been for daily use, what remains to us is largely the legacy of the ceremonies and rituals attached to the burying of the distinguished dead. We see prized and superior examples, specially made for the occasion, alongside ordinary, everyday pots.

In this early pre-wheel pottery, whether for daily or ceremonial use, there is an enormous variety of shape and decoration – and a great range of clay, from the light, plastic, burnished red body of the Egyptian to the hard, almost stoneware Kansu and the stony, rough bonfired pots of Bronze Age Britain.

Identification

Sometimes a hand-built pot declares itself by its scale or shape – it may have a round bottom, a leaning, 'wonky' appearance, a bulging silhouette – or by its thinness or texture. Very often, however, it is not easy to identify from its appearance whether a pot is hand-built or thrown, and if hand-built, by what method. Generally the more careful and skilful the potter the more difficult it is to say. Even if the forming has left scratches and indentations, the subsequent surface treatment often eliminates all evidence of this: polishing will destroy tool marks, slips will cover all evidence of previous working. It is the carelessly or crudely made piece, where surface has not been obliterated by scraping and smoothing, or where the joining of coils has been imperfectly carried out – leading to cracks and fractures – that reveals most. There is a small chunk of fired clay in the Bronze

Age section of the National Museum of Wales which shows a break where a coil has been badly joined. It adds conviction to conjecture as to how the Bronze Age beaker was formed.

Ware which has been damaged during firing is often called 'wasters', and it is through these waste products that the manufacturing technique is most clearly seen. It is only now

Pre-dynastic Egyptian cinerary urn, burnished earthenware. 53 cm.

Medieval jug found at White Castle, Kent. Late 13th Century.

becoming apparent, through the excavation of kiln sites, that coil-built pottery was produced in large quantities in many parts of Britain in the Middle Ages. For there are no contemporary records: 'potters were peasants keeping no records themselves and generally appearing only as names in tax lists or rent rolls.'* The pot of the Middle Ages has been described by a contemporary medievalist thus: 'it is cheap, usually common and survives well in the ground.'* Because pots were cheap and common the wealthy, those most likely to provide documentary evidence, scarcely mentioned the material although vessels in other materials are frequently referred to in accounts. However, the reeves' draft accounts, the medical, craftsmen, and, less commonly, cookery recipes of the time

*from *Medieval Pottery of the Oxford Region* (see Bibliography)

did show the multiplicity of purposes to which the earthenware vessels were put.

The common ceramic forms of Medieval England were the cooking pot, the jug and the bowl. The cooking pot was used not only for cooking – many of those found are not sooty and have clearly not been near a fire – but as all-purpose containers. Earthenware jugs were used for heating water for the stews and bath-houses; bowls were used for washing clothes. Other earthenware vessels were purchased for butter and cheese-making, and infirmaries bought earthenware pots for use in monastic hospitals. Garden pots, preserving jars and building ornaments also made use of the potter's craft and pots were even built into churches to improve the acoustics.

This versatility of the common form can be seen in Neolithic times and in tribal societies, where the object may be in everyday common use and also used for ceremony or ritual: the burial urn is the container, the ceremonial feast pot is the cooking utensil. The names given by archaeologists – beakers, food vessels, cinerary urns, pigmy cups – are used to classify, not to describe purpose; to take these names literally is to limit and confuse. We cannot know how these shapes were used by prehistoric man: as with Medieval pots one form might be used for several purposes. Conversely, many differing shapes might be used for the same purpose; we have only to compare the burial urns of the Egyptians, Etruscans and the Chinese to realise this. But while it is difficult to know the *use* of the historic pot, the way the pot was *made* is even harder to discover and our knowledge is largely limited to what we can learn from inspecting the artefacts themselves and by considering those societies where hand-building is still used.

Ethnic potters today

In Africa, in Meso-America, in Papua New Guinea and in other underdeveloped parts of the world, hand-building is still used even though the wheel, in however primitive a form, was developed as early as 4000–3000 B.C. To understand why this is so we must blot out our twentieth century values and concepts, and our scale and image of the world as we know it. Quite often groups retain their traditional way of working, even where the wheel is known, for a technical reason. The local clay, coiled or hand-built, can be fired in a bonfire to make pots suitable in shape and texture for use in cooking over an open fire. They can be made cheaply and quickly – firing may take only half an hour – and the method requires no capital equipment.

Even though time may have no economic value in such societies, the techniques used to make the pot are very efficient indeed. The Sokoto potters of Nigeria, tamping in a hollow in the ground, have been observed to form the body of a round water pot in 3–5 minutes. Michael Cardew has described the Yoruba tradition in the large town of Ilorin in northern Nigeria as being so highly organised that it can almost be called mass-production by hand. The Mexicans and other Meso-Americans use moulds with incised designs carved into them as rapidly as a wheel thrower might throw similar forms.

Interacting with these highly evolved techniques is a social content which is all-important, and a part of the social fabric of a group.

The actual *making* may be formalised and social. The woman of the household may make pots as they are needed, as part of the domestic routine. It may be sporadic, if firing can be carried out only in the dry season.

Or men and women may work together: for example, the Pueblo pottery is made by the women while the men dig the clay and decorate. In Thailand the men build, and the women decorate and do the light work. In south Belize the Mayan potters are women over thirty, while in Ghana it is the young Ashanti women who make the pots. In Indonesia the whole village contributes towards the production of pots.

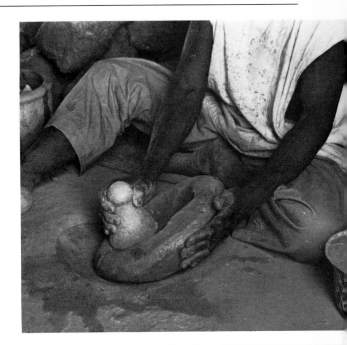

(Above) *Starting the form by tamping in a hollow in the ground, while slowly rotating the thick mass of clay.*

(Below) *Moche vessel moulded in the form of two birds. Peru, 25 cm.*

Wassau cult object shaped like a pot with added face and head, pointed, closed base and openings for mouth and eyes. East and west Sepik province, Papua New Guinea.

Large, ceremonial common cooking pot. Sepik River Kwamo, Papua New Guinea.

In the Mayrik area of Sepik in Papua New Guinea, the men are responsible for the artistic endeavour, and while they make cult figures for a secret society the women make the clay cooking pots. In some villages in the area the women make a common eating bowl while the men make or decorate ceremonial vessels.

The *using* may also be socially significant. While most of the pots may be utilitarian there does seem to be a vital ritual element which accounts for some of the pot making in tribal society. An example is the musical pot made and played by an Ibibio women's society. Another, also from Ibibioland (south-eastern Nigeria), is the large ceremonial pot used to contain palm wine at ceremonial functions such as marriages and funerals – a communal possession, it may be kept in a special hut alongside other ritual objects.

In Papua, too, there is a large, common ceremonial cooking pot, 30–50 centimetres high, used in men's houses during special feasts and during cult ceremonies such as initiation. Sometimes pot making within a group is a means of gaining individual or collective prestige. The techniques may be highly secret and this helps to give a very strong identity to a group.

Sometimes pottery is used in exchange and barter, and around the trading systems there may be, as in the Amphlett islands of New Guinea, seasonal feasts and celebrations; a central event here in the lives of the Motu pot makers takes place around the Hiri trading system.

Pots may even – though rarely – be wealth objects, set aside as a bride's dowry. This is so in New Britain in the Umboi islands (off the coast of Papua New Guinea). In one village, Kawi, thirty-five pots were owned by one home and only two were used as cooking pots. In such areas more pots are likely to be found among a man's store of valuables than among his wife's working vessels.

We see that pottery in these small, disappearing communities in various parts of the world is all of a piece with the traditional style of living. Whether the objects fabricated are cheap, disposable and mundane, or

Ikwa Umanah scraping an Ibibio musical pot which she has just made.

treasured, decorated ritual objects, whether they are useful or symbolic, the making of them is so much part of the cultural fabric that to change procedures could destroy the mores of a society. That this way of life has survived into the latter part of the twentieth century is due to the strength of tradition, and to the fact that some of these groups are so isolated that there has been no interruption in their view of the world for centuries. In Papua New Guinea, the central Highlands were not penetrated until 1930, some areas of the country were unknown until 1950, and some small nomadic tribes were encountered only in the last ten years. There is a tribe in Yunnan in China making pots as they were made in prehistoric times. Inevitably these social groups, and others like them, are becoming extinct. Yet because of their survival into the twentieth century there are contemporary records, consisting of eye-witness accounts, photographs, films and artefacts, all of which explain working methods. And as pottery is still made within a tradition which discourages individuality and innovation, we can make reasonable assumptions about the techniques of the earliest users of clay.

The contemporary potter

The potter of today has not inherited his craft, he is not even an essential part of the social needs of his community, he does not fulfil a practical necessity. He has chosen to work as he does. Unlike that of the traditional potter his work is stamped by innovation and individuality. We are able to recognise the

21

Ruth Duckworth: asymmetrical stoneware pot.

maker when we see his work, whether he is called a domestic potter, a ceramic sculptor, a craftsman potter or a studio potter. He may work within a tradition, say that of the country potter, or of the Japanese through Bernard Leach; he may work outside tradition, trying to assimilate the fashion and attitudes of the age in which he lives, or he may attempt to make something which has meaning outside common understanding.

If we were to ask a traditional potter why he works in clay the answer would be inevitable and self-evident. If we ask the potter today, his answer will be essentially of the twentieth century – even though the work may derive from the past, or from an alien cultural tradition.

Coiling is the earliest and most traditional form of pottery. So why do potters choose to work in this way today? The answer is mainly an aesthetic one, and practical considerations arise only to reach the desired result.

It allows me to: 'build thin forms'
      'make large pots'
      'make large pots which should convey a sense of organic growth, wholeness and sensuality'

It gives: 'quality of form and a technique that gives a strong bond for the raku firing'
      'a greater control and the possibility of asymmetry'

It has already been noted that coiling is a practical way to build and control large forms.

One contemporary potter quoted above has mentioned thinness as a feature he wishes to incorporate. Thin forms have been made in the past where there has been suitable clay: for example, the Badarian bowls of pre-dynastic Egypt are egg-shell thin. But we can now choose our material, choose what we wish to make and the means to realise this choice.

'Organic growth' has been noted as a quality of coiled pots. Of all methods this is indeed the most organic, for it does not easily lend itself to precision and can lead to a vitality of form, an idiosyncratic individuality which is attractively alive. It is the twentieth century that enunciates and delights in this quality. I doubt whether the African potter sought, or was even aware of it, in his huge rounded pots which were so like the fruits and gourds around him.

Asymmetry is a possibility of this technique. Pots are naturally circular in cross-section – this is inevitable in throwing, and normal in coiling and hand-building. It requires a conscious effort to exploit the imprecisions of coiling, or to control the building in such a way as to produce something with asymmetry, only partial symmetry or none at all.

'Coiling is all or nothing. It is merely a manual skill of getting the clay into place,' says one potter. Whether we see coiling as a means to an end, quite simply a technique that serves our ideas, or whether our concepts have been evolved and stimulated through the technique, we do have to gain some measure of technical mastery before either approach can be fully satisfied. In succeeding chapters we shall see how this can be achieved.

(Opposite) *Pot by Gabrielle Koch with an organic quality achieved through the process of making and firing.*

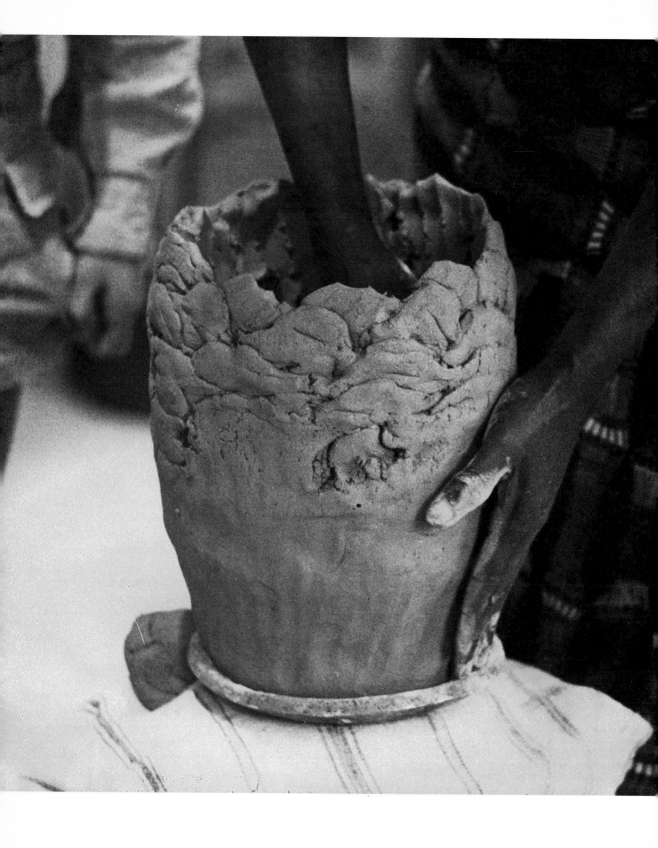

2

Starting the pot

Hand-building requires few ingredients – clay, water, hands and the simplest of tools. Like throwing it needs great co-ordination, but it is relatively slow and encourages deliberation and conscious decision while the form is being made. Perhaps it is because it is technically simple, and because the shape is under control at all stages that clear thinking is necessary.

The clay

It has been said that any clay is good provided one is willing to learn to use it. Bernard Leach says: 'Don't be too particular about your clay. You need certain temperature resistance and you want sufficient plasticity . . . but be satisfied within those limits with what your district produces because even for a second-rate clay there can be a first-class treatment.'*

However, the type of clay that is used considerably affects the character of the pot. The pottery of Bronze Age man, like that of ethnic groups today, was made from the clay they found: the ware might be thick and heavy, or delicate and fine-bodied; white, red, grey or buff; smooth and silky to the touch or rough and stony. All these qualities – plasticity, colour and texture – are inherent in the material.

*from *The Potter's Challenge* (see Bibliography)

Nigerian potter Ladi Kwali has hollowed out the lump to which she is adding pieces of clay.

But it would be misleading to think that early man used clay just as it was dug. The pottery made now by peoples whose civilisation is classified as 'Stone Age' shows their understanding of the practical necessities of clay and its preparation, even though they may not understand the underlying technology. For example, the traditional culture of Papua New Guinea is Stone Age – there was no knowledge of metal until Europeans came. Experience taught the Papuans the need to add an 'opener' (discussed below) to their clay, but their reasons for choosing a particular material were clouded with superstition. Those who lived near the shore believed that only salty sand could be used; those living inland thought that only their sand was suitable: in fact, both worked equally well.

The methods used by two potters described by Ann Woods in her research papers – who happen to be a man and a woman from different areas of the Kavango region of northern south-west Africa – illustrate how clay might be prepared in a non-technological society.

The man uses clay from a dry flood plain of the river, digging it out with an adze axe. The woman gathers her clay in the wet state from the river. Both refine their clay, but in quite different ways. The man pounds the dry clay with a pestle into lumps less than 1 centimetre in size until all visible organic matter is removed; it is then soaked. The woman refines

25

approximate proportions of two parts of grog to three parts of clay. The clay is now ready to be used.

Such grogged clay, ready for immediate use, can be fired successfully in an open flame. Pottery which is fired without a kiln is always made of clay incorporating some kind of opener – sometimes known also as 'temper' or 'filler'. It may be mineral – such as grog, fire-clay, sand or mica in the form of volcanic ash, or it may be organic – sawdust, sponge spicules, plant fibres, feathers, chopped straw, cow or sheep dung, shells, millet chaff. The mineral content leads to a stronger pot because organic material burns away during firing, leaving small holes. Of mineral fillers experiment has shown that sand gives the weakest body and sherd the strongest.

Most of us today will make use of clay carefully prepared by the manufacturers and supplied in plastic bags. It will be malleable and ready for use as it is. There are a variety of clay bodies available and they will be chosen according to the scale and type of work. Manufacturers' catalogues give descriptions of their prepared clays which include basic information about texture, colour, firing range, vitrification point and suitable uses: for beginners this is a good starting point. There are clays that are already heavily grogged, such as a 'Crank' mixture, or a 'raku' clay, and fine clays such as a red earthenware, a bone china or a porcelain.

Most hand-builders will want to use a clay that has a 'bite' to it and may need to add more opener to the clay bought. For a small amount the best way is to scatter a bench with the dampened opener (unless the clay is sticky and wet and needs to be dried) and to knead the clay on it. As the clay is worked it will pick up the grains, which will eventually become integrated with the clay. If a large amount is to be mixed by hand it is probably quicker to 'sandwich slice' the clay and scatter the dampened filler between the slices, wedging and kneading conveniently-sized pieces cut from across the grain of the sandwich until the mixture is even. For those who are lucky enough to own a

Ibibio potter, Ikwa Umanah, mixing the opener and preparing the clay body by trampling on it (1972).

her wet clay by hand, removing large objects such as stones, twigs, roots or leaves by squashing small handfuls of clay between finger and thumb.

After this both proceed in the same way. Old sherds – broken pieces of fired clay – are pounded with a pestle to make the opener, 'grog', which is then added to the clay in pugmill – which will amalgamate the mix mechanically – rough kneading followed by 'pugging' is easiest of all.

Whether a clay is bought with the opener already added, or whether the potter adds his own, there are clear practical reasons for its inclusion:

1. It makes a highly plastic clay easier to work and less sticky to handle; of course, too much grog will so reduce the plasticity that the mixture will be unworkable.

2. It reduces shrinking and allows the pot to dry more evenly, reducing the risk of cracking.

3. It reduces shrinkage during firing. This factor is not significant in most open (or bonfire) firings, which are unlikely to reach temperatures at which shrinkage occurs.

4. It helps to prevent breakage and bursting during the firing. This is particularly important in bonfire firing where, as long as the body is coarse enough, the pot will come through intact. A coarse-bodied pot will also have good resistance to thermal shock when used in cooking.

Clearly the kind of firing to be carried out is important in the choice of clay. Clays which vitrify at 1200°C, or above are suitable for an 'earthenware' firing; for a 'stoneware' firing a slowly maturing clay which will stand a high temperature without deformation is needed, and for the type of firing where the pot is in contact with the flames, or for a raku firing, an open clay which has the capacity to withstand thermal shock is necessary. The various practices of contemporary potters illustrate how important the kind of firing, and therefore the choice of clay, is to their work.

Gabrielle Koch, who low fires her pots to 900°C, uses a mixture of red earthenware and a heavily grogged clay such as a raku mixture, both bought ready made up.

Monica Young fires her very large pots to 1300°C, and uses a Crank body which has a low shrinkage rate and a high vitrification point.

Kneading the grog into the clay.
Mixing clays
a. a sandwich, sliced to show layers of two clays and grog
b. rough-kneaded part of the sandwich
c. the same (b) sliced to show the mixture
d. the final 'sausage'

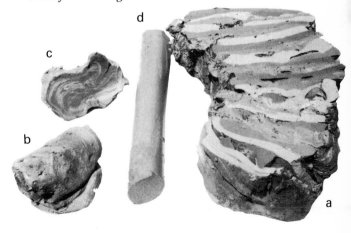

(Left) *Red burnished earthenware pitcher from Bronze Age Cyprus. 42 cm. c. 2500 B.C.*

(Right) *Red burnished earthenware double-spouted jug from Cyprus. 24·5 cm. 2100–2000 B.C.*

David Roberts 'rakus' his pots – a process which requires the pot to be withdrawn from the kiln while it is still red hot – so he must use a clay which will withstand thermal shock. He uses a St Thomas white clay to which is added a medium grog (20s to dust).

Ewen Henderson uses whatever clay is available – bone china, porcelain, Crank, stoneware. He often combines a variety of clays in one form, firing to a temperature of 1260°C.

He is not concerned with predictability or even safety during firing: his approach is totally experimental. He says he will try anything remotely plastic, for each clay has it limitations and he likes to fire to destruction point.

Forming the base

The form of the base always was of practical importance. If the pot was to be used for cooking in the embers of the fire it was best to make it round-bottomed: it would then sit comfortably and the flame would lick evenly round the curve, reducing the risk of thermal shock. In a culture without furniture, storage vessels too would be round-bottomed because they could be rested in soil or sand. But if there were flat surfaces the vessels would be sturdily based and flat-bottomed.

The storage ware – jugs, jars, amphora – from Cyprus illustrate this and show that changes took place not only in taste but in the amenities of the homes where they were used. Over a long period of transition, between 2500 and 1600 B.C., the flat-bottomed vessels belonging to a society where there were shelves, well-made tables and level, paved floors, were slowly replaced, surprisingly, by round-bottomed vessels – suggesting rougher homes where pots would be rested in hollows scraped in the earth floors.

Making the base is technically quite difficult and it is not surprising that many different methods have been used – some more suitable for round bottoms and some for flat bottoms. Indeed, few pots are made entirely by coiling, and it is most often at the start, the forming of the base, that other techniques are incorporated. As we shall see, these are many and various.

1. The base may itself be <u>coiled.</u> A sausage of clay (how this is made will be dealt with in the next chapter) is coiled into a spiral, starting from the centre and continuing until the desired diameter of the base is achieved. This may be done on a flat board, in a shallow dish, or on the lap, with no other support – as is done in Fiji and in Ibibioland. Or, unusually, as in the Morobe Province of Papua New Guinea, the coil may be rolled on its side; here a short length is left sticking out to form the typical point, or 'nipple', in the centre of the base.

The coils are bonded by dragging the fingers across the clay to close any gaps and to smooth the surface. The method does not seem to be

(Top right) *Ikwa Umanah forming the base of a pot by spiral building. Note rough coils and unfinished pots in the background (1972).*

(Right) *Kesesa from Morobe Province, Papua New Guinea, rolling up the first coil to form the base.*

common: it carries with it the danger of poor joining and is not as quick as other ways.

2. The pot may be started with a <u>disc of clay</u>. A ball is flattened between the palms of the hands or on a flat surface, or rolled out with a rolling pin, and a disc of as even a thickness as possible cut out, either freely or by using a template.

(Inset) *Peter Stoodley flattening a disc of clay rolled out with rolling pin.*

(Below) *Pueblo potter Maria Martinez flattening a sheet of clay using the whole hand, fingers and palms. Note pots drying, removed from their moulds, and the bowl with grog at her side (1948).*

3. In the above two methods the pot starts with a base upon which coils are to be added to create the form. But the base and the start of the wall can be made in one process by starting with a ball of clay, pushing the thumb into the centre and <u>pinching</u> up the clay. This can be done quickly: if a number of 'pinch pots' are made at one time their bases can be allowed to stiffen before coils are added. It is often best to leave the pot, inverted, on its rim until the base has dried sufficiently to retain its shape.

4. A flat sheet of clay may be beaten, rolled, or pressed between palm and fingers and modelled into a disc, then laid into a <u>mould</u> – it may be

(Right) *Magdalene Odundo pinching the base of a pot.*

a gourd, a calabash, a broken pot base, a specially biscuit-fired saucer, a basket, a plaster mould, or even a hollow in the ground. In most cases the mould can act not only as a support but also as a means of turning the vessel as it is being formed. American Indians use a small, previously fired saucer of about 12 centimetres diameter and about 1 centimetre thickness called a 'puki'. Occasionally two are used back to back to form a turntable. I sometimes use a deep plaster mould; when it is firm enough the moulded clay is withdrawn, then pinched and scraped into a new form.

An alternative method is to place the sheet of clay on the outside of the mould, which may be an inverted pot. Michael Cardew describes how this is done in the Yoruba town of Ilorin. The woman potter first treads out the prepared clay into a rough sheet. Dampening the bottom of an old, inverted pot she sprinkles wood ash on it to prevent the clay sticking, then places the flattened clay on it. Using a small beater she thins and stretches the clay to cover about half the surface of the mould; water is sprinkled and ash scattered on it as it grows. After the clay is compressed by rubbing a corn cob over the surface, and the edge has been trimmed, the pot is left to dry until it is stiff enough to be lifted off; it is then rested on its rim until dry enough to be built upon.

In the small Chinese town of Tung Kwan on the Xiang Jiang river the lower halves of large storage vessels, about 60 centimetres high, are built up from beaten clay shapes draped in sections over a cloth-covered mould.

5. The two above examples have introduced another important technique – the use of <u>paddle and anvil.</u> The paddle is a beating tool, which may be a bat or a stone, while the anvil, which supports the clay on the other side, may be a mushroom-shaped object of fired clay, a rounded stone, a hand or a mould.

Unlike the Ilorin potter just described, who beats the clay on the outside of an inverted pot to make it grow, the Darfur of the Sudan use the

(Left) *Maria Martinez placing the sheet of clay into a mould.*

The clay form after it is removed from the deep plaster mould.

The moulded form is pinched and scraped into a wide, bowl-like base.

33

Mallam Garba from Nigeria pounding the soft clay with a stone pestle as he turns it in the anvil.

the whole oval shape of a water jar is formed in this way; finally a coil is added to make the neck. It is known as the 'Dundunge' method and is practised by Mallam Garba, a Muslim potter from north central Nigeria whom we shall mention again. He embeds a fired, shallow bowl in the ground as the anvil.

The paddle and anvil technique used in conjunction with coiling is also found among the American Indians: the Yunan, Piman and Shoshonean potters. The universal water container of the continent of India, a wide-necked round-bottomed vessel, is made by throwing a narrow pot and beating it when leather-hard. A small mushroom-shaped clay anvil is pressed against the inner wall by one hand while the other beats against it on the outside with a concave wooden paddle.

6. The most direct, and perhaps the least sophisticated, method is to start with a lump of clay and simply p<u>ull</u> it up. The best-known exponent of this technique is Ladi Kwali, an African potter who worked with Michael Cardew at the Pottery Training Centre at Abuja, Nigeria; through him she visited and demonstrated the 'Gwari' way of making a water pot in Europe and America.

Working on a circular drum about 40 centimetres high she places a lump of clay in a saucer-shaped calabash supported by a ring of grass or cloth. Standing as she works she pounds and punches the clay with her fist to form a hollow. When it is deep enough and the bottom is of the right thickness she moves slowly around the pot, dragging the clay up with her finger tips, producing a straight-sided pot with irregular walls, marked inside with slightly diagonal finger marks. The rim too is irregular and pelleted with clay which has been pulled up (see p. 24). The moving, pulling and thinning continues until the walls are of the right thickness. Then, without waiting for the clay to stiffen, she begins coiling.

opposite technique: the beating is applied inside and the supporting anvil is outside – a depression in the ground covered with matting and powdered with dry donkey dung to prevent sticking. The form grows thinner and wider as the beating and turning process is repeated. A bowl-like form, the lower half of a pot, is formed roughly and quickly. A smaller pestle of fired clay is then used to refine the form. The pot is set aside on its rim to harden before coils are added.

With minor variations this is a classic way of forming and thinning clay. It is the method used in the Muslim state of Sokoto in the north of Nigeria by the Hausa men potters, where almost

(Right) *Ladi Kwali from Nigeria pressing down on the solid lump of clay placed in the calabash mould.*

Turntables from Thrapsano, Crete, used to make pithoi. Note cut out bank (1981).

7. The base may be <u>thrown</u> on a wheel. In Thrapsano in Crete, large earthenware jars for storing oil, wine and cereals have been made in this way for three thousand years. These thick-walled pithoi were found in the Bronze Age Palace of Minos at Knossos, dating from the Middle Minoan period, somewhere between 2000 and 1700 B.C. Such a pot, of average size, would hold about 160 litres.

Once – and for a long time – this was a thriving industry. In 1910 archaeologists excavating the Palace of Minos rode out to watch itinerant potters making pithoi – such as

(Left) Large 'Medallion pithos' found in the Minoan Palace at Knossos. Although jars like this were mainly used for storage, they were also often used as burial urns.

they had just found – on the slopes of Mount Juktas; in 1975 the potters Michael and Sheila Casson found only a few families, no longer itinerant, still making pots, and only two men making the large pithoi.

Fortunately in 1970 Maria Voyatzoglou had recorded these pots being made by teams in a very organised way. Traditionally, groups of six men formed a guild, each having his own task. There was the master potter, the second potter, the wheeler, the clay man, the wood cutter and the carrier. They were, at that time, itinerant and combined farming with potting.

The pots were made on a turntable set into a ditch where there would be eight to twelve such wheel heads about two feet apart. Small, square spaces were cut to broaden the trench so that the wheeler could sit cross-legged, facing a turntable. He caused it to rotate by pushing and pulling a wooden bar fixed horizontally through the axle on which the wheel was set. The master potter sat on the ground opposite the wheeler

37

From Beit Shebab, Lebanon; thrown bases after beating (1965).

Lydia from Wanigela, Papua New Guinea, pushing a ring of clay down from her prepared lump.

(Below) *Thinning and pulling up the first ring.*

but at a higher level. In that position he could centre the clay revolving on the wheel. As the pot grew he would sit higher and higher until finally he stood to form the lip. The first section and the base would be thrown together from a cake of clay patted on to the wheel head, with two coils of clay joined or 'luted' to it.

Potters from Beit Shebab in the Lebanon also combine throwing and coiling. Like the Cretans these potters too are men, and they make large storage jars for wine, arak, oil, olives, rice and conserves, using a technique which may have changed little since 2000 B.C. But their method is totally different. They start by forming the clay into a tall cone, about 20 centimetres in diameter at the base and 50 centimetres tall. From this 'hump' six or seven conical bowls are thrown to form the bases of the larger jars. When these are leather-hard they are dipped in slip, and using the paddle and anvil method are beaten into rounded bowls with thin rims, and left to dry. Their paddle is rather like a thick table-tennis bat, and the anvil is a thick wooden disc covered with cloth and carrying a strap to keep it in place on the left hand. Later these are used again in the shaping process (see p. 58).

8. In a village in Wanigela, Papua New Guinea, there is a strange, eccentric way of making the base and pot which seems to be unique. From a cylinder of clay a ring is pulled down to the

base and then dragged up; the central clay cylinder is used to make the coils, and finally the base is scraped to remove all traces of the original lump of clay.

Building a pot upside down and forming its base at the end is surprisingly widespread, a method found in different times and different places and including variations which involve many of the foregoing techniques.

First, a thick coil of clay (sometimes formed by laying two or three one upon the other) is laid in a ring on a board, then drawn up and

Rolling coils from handfuls of clay taken from the central lump, she overlaps and joins them to the rim.

(Below left) *Lydia consolidating the inside with her knuckles.*

(Below) *Gladys scraping the ridge around the base.*

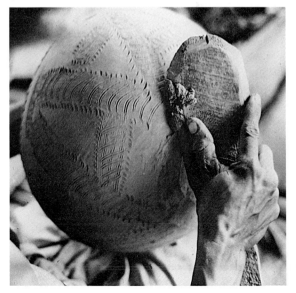

The potter from the Amphlett Islands beating the bowl that she has formed upside down.

The clay is thinned and beaten gently until the form is closed. Note the partly formed pot in the background drying before further beating can take place.

pulled inward by the fingers. Building is continued, sometimes by coiling, sometimes by paddle and anvil, and sometimes totally by pulling and pinching, until the right size for the mouth is reached, when a rim is added. As soon as the neck will support it the half pot is turned

over, giving the shape of an open bowl, and building is continued either by drawing in the thick clay which was formerly at the bottom, or by adding coils – making the opening progressively smaller – until it is no longer possible to get the hand inside. The hole is closed by adding a small coil or by beating the clay.

The Vume of Ghana use coils to extend the pot, while the Ashanti of Ghana make the whole pot by hollowing out and dragging up a solid lump of clay. In Guatajiagua in Salvador the vessel is totally pulled up from the clay cylinder except that a small coil is used to close the base, and sometimes another coil to form the rim. In Sri Lanka, thrown pots are cut off the hump without bases, then beaten with paddle and anvil to close the bottom. The Papuan potter from the Amphlett Islands has formed her bowl from slabs and rough handfuls of short, rough coils; she beats and thins it, using her hand as an anvil. The earliest Jōman (Japanese) cooking pots – at least as early as 3000 B.C. – have pointed or round bottoms and it is thought that they were built upside down with broad ribbons of clay until flat bases and wavy rims became fashionable in the early Jōman period.

Bernard Leach was puzzled by the fact that many Medieval pots had rounded bottoms, and conjectured that the only practical way in which they could have been made was by making a pot without a base and then 'stitching' one on. Recent research suggests that this may indeed be so.

All the methods described above for making the base are traditional: they require great skill and judgement, as any experiments with an unfamiliar method will show. Where experience is most needed is in assessing how far a particular operation can be continued: how far the lump of clay can be pulled and stretched before it collapses; how the depth of clay remaining can be judged so that the base is neither too thick nor too thin; how the pot may be pounded so that the wall is equally thick all over; how much more stress the clay can take; whether the clay is wet or dry enough. Questions such as these point to the difficulties; each of us

Medieval unglazed cooking pot from the site of the Benedictine Abbey of Tewkesbury. 13th–14th Century.

answers by tactile intuition gained by experience.

Most people who are taught to coil learn by building on a disc, coil by coil. Because this method is made up of distinct stages it is possible to be in control throughout. It is not only a good starting point but can become a highly developed technique. Contemporary potters who use it are David Roberts, Monica Young and Peter Stoodley: they roll out the clay and form coils directly upon it. Helen Pincombe, who bases her technique on that of the Pueblo Indians, beats out a ball between her hands while turning it, then flattens it into a disc and starts coiling.

Other contemporary potters start in different ways. John Ward forms the base by pinching and hollowing out a ball of clay in the hand. Ewen Henderson, whose methods are very varied, usually uses the pinch technique for the base. Gabrielle Koch and Magdalene Odundo use moulds – both make round-bottomed pots. Gabrielle starts with a slab which she places in a round mould, and Magdalene pinches a pot before placing it into a gourd or biscuit-fired form. The American potter Kenneth Beittel combines throwing with his own brand of coiling. He may throw the base, the base and lip, or just the lip.

Once a particular approach is reasonably under control it is a good idea to try other ways of starting the work. Even though the clay dictates its own terms you are the manipulator; if it is handled sensitively and with full regard to its nature, *anything* that works for you can be used. There can be no precise recipe for the making of a good pot. It is not possible to say, for example, how to position oneself. The Ibibio women sit on the floor; the Pueblo Indian potter Maria Martinez knelt; David Roberts sits at a table; Gabrielle Koch stands. Some potters walk around their pots, others turn them in their formers, while others use a turntable. Neither is it possible to say exactly how to place the hands; each potter intuitively finds a way of handling the material which is natural and in keeping with the desired process.

But both hands always play a part, sometimes working equally, sometimes with one or other dominant. Often the whole hand, from the tips of the fingers to the base of the palm, is put to use; sometimes only the pads of the fingers are used, or just the palms. The hand can become a cup to mould as the other pinches, or it can become a weight to pound the clay, or a paddle to beat it. The hands may work aggressively, crudely punching, pulling or beating; at other times they may work with extreme delicacy, gently persuading, extending, or finalising. There is no mystique: all is discovered in the making.

3

Adding to the base

As we have seen, the way the base has been made may already have begun to determine the shape of the pot. There to build upon is a flat surface, a low-walled form, a bowl, or even a large open shape which is already half a pot. On to these clay is to be added: the obvious way is by coiling.

Making the coils

It is possible to make very regular coils by extruding them from a pugmill. However, making by hand is more common, and for the ethnic potter it is the only way. In one method a lump of clay is slapped and squeezed into a rough sausage shape – the less finger-indented the better. On a clean, slightly dampened flat surface, with the fingers of both hands outspread, the clay sausage is rolled back and forth, at first gently – so that the clay becomes rounded in cross-section – then with a slight pressure which will cause it to lengthen. Starting from the middle the hands must constantly move along the length of the rope, pressing it slightly to the flat surface, but not so heavily as to flatten the coil. The length and diameter aimed at depend on the size of the pot and the thickness of the wall desired. The more

plastic the clay – and skilful the potter – the more slender the coil that can be made. The ideal coil has a uniform diameter along its length and requires quite a lot of skill and judgement in the making. Such a coil, laid on an even rim, can produce a very regular form – if that is the aim.

In imagining this procedure the picture is perhaps of someone standing and working at a table or workbench. But coils are rolled in some societies where work is carried out at ground level. In Ibibioland in south-east Nigeria the potter sits on the ground, with legs stretched out on either side of a board on which she can roll out the rough coils already moulded in the hand. In Papua New Guinea roughly rolled-out coils are stretched to lengths between 15 and 120 centimetres, using the heel and palm of the hand only.

More commonly, ethnic groups will use another method of forming coils in which a rough sausage of clay is squeezed between the fingers and then rolled between the hands vertically. It is the method of the traditional Gwari style of Nigeria demonstrated by Ladi Kwali. The Pueblo Indians, represented by Maria Martinez, also extrude coils vertically from a ball rolled between the palms of the hands.

Although coils formed in this way may not be as smooth-sided or as meticulously even as those made on a flat surface, they can be quite regular and controlled, and are well suited to the

(Left) *Maria Martinez forming a coil, squeezing it gently from the ball of clay (1950).*

Ikwa Umanah squeezing clay into a roughed coil.

(Above right) *Ikwa Umanah rolling the clay into a coil on the dampened board; she breaks off the splayed, useless end.*

organic growth of a form which is to be continuously modelled. In a society where furniture is unimportant and minimal, the method is natural: it is a quick way anywhere but it does need considerable judgement and

skill to produce a coil of useful thickness and length.

Building with coils

There are many ways in which coils may be added to the base. Most often they are added singly by placing them on the rim, one hand

(Right) *Ladi Kwali rolling a coil between the palms of her hands.*

44

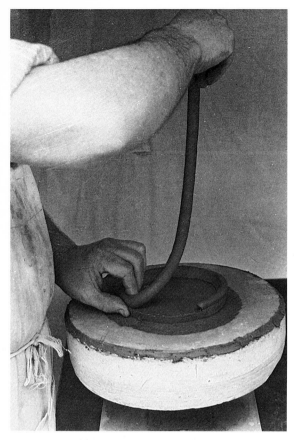

Peter Stoodley guiding and firming the first coil on a cut disc base.

Peter Stoodley pulling the coil down to join it to the base.

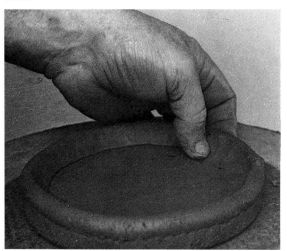

guiding and the other hand placing. At the same time the right hand will often pull the new clay over the clay below, exerting gentle pressure with finger and thumb to bond the coil firmly to the rim. The coil is broken off when a ring is complete.

Sometimes two or three coils may be placed consecutively on top of each other so that several are joined at the same time. Or a long length of clay can be laid helically (usually referred to as 'spiral building') on the pot rim – that is, literally 'coiled on'. This is one of the main methods used by the Papuans and it is why some of their coils are made as long as 120 centimetres. They may not be joined until the pot is nearly 40 centimetres high, when they are bonded inside and out by dragging the thumb from top to bottom. One long coil,

David Roberts pressing the coil on to the top of the rim.

Ikwa Umanah thinning the coil as she adds it to the rim.

'spiralled' on itself, may be all that is needed to complete the main part of the vessel.

Coils may be pressed directly from the top to make a positive contact, leaving a dimpled row of impressions. David Roberts applies his extruded coils in this way: placing them loosely he uses coils up to about 1 centimetre in diameter, which do not necessarily cover the

whole circumference, and presses two or three rows upon each other before joining them with deft pulls inside and outside.

The Ibibio potter illustrates that the coil which has been rolled out on the board may be squeezed and thinned further at the moment that it is pressed on to the rim.

Often the rope of clay is placed below the rim and overlapping by as much as half or even – as in the case of the Indians of San Ildefonso – by threequarters of what is to be applied. This overlapping method is probably the best way to

start for it has the advantage of giving a greater surface for bonding, and thus less likelihood of cracking along the joint. It is generally recommended that the overlapping coil should be placed inside the growing form, leaning slightly inward, particularly in the early stages, to prevent flaring.

Coiling, much slower than throwing, and slower than other hand-building processes, is essentially rhythmical; at no time is this more evident than in the bonding. The whole circumference must be methodically circled as the clay from the new coil is pulled down to the partly formed pot – either by turning the pot or by moving around it. The regular motions of the hands are defined clearly by the graceful pacing of those ethnic potters who walk backward around their pots as though in a stately dance. Although bonding is usually done after the coil is sited, the two are sometimes combined. The Indians of the Yucatan, Mexico, for example, feed the clay with the right hand into the interior of the pot with repeated short rotations of the wrist, spreading it as it is applied with the extended index finger. As the clay is highly plastic the effect is almost as though it is being smeared along the growing vessel.

Sometimes the marks of the thumb-dragged or tool-pulled clay are visible by design or accident. More often they will be scraped or beaten away. Occasionally the coils are bonded – and perhaps scraped – only inside the pot and remain visible on the outside.

Variations

One might suppose that the diameter of the coil defines the amount by which the pot grows in height with its application, and defines also the thickness of the wall. But the coil may be thinned and heightened even before it is added. John Ward, for example, flattens his bench-rolled coils on a plaster 'bat' with his thumb, then smooths them with a metal kidney scraper, finishing with a strip 7–8 centimetres deep.

(Left) *Magdalene Odundo overlapping the coil on the outside of the ingoing pot, thumbing it firmly into place.*

Terra-cotta unglazed pot by Michael Hullis. The coils are joined on the inside only while the outside coils are placed so that the joining point of each forms a diagonal feature. 46 cm.

John Ward adding a flattened coil to a bowl form.

49

Mallam Garba luting a thick coil of soft clay mixed with dry donkey dung to the dampened rim of his pot.

(Middle right) *The neck is squeezed to thin and shape it.*

The Beit Shebab potter flattening and stretching his coil as he applies it in a spiral on to the beaten bowl base. He works at a stone table; there are several in the workshop at different heights, used for different processes.

Gabrielle Koch also flattens her coils. The pot may also be made to grow further if the new clay is flattened, drawn up, pinched, modelled or even thrown on a wheel during bonding. The potters of Beit Shebab, applying their hand-rolled coils 75 centimetres long and 4 centimetres thick in a diminishing spiral, press and heighten each coil as it is placed. Later it will be heightened further.

The Cretan second potter of Thrapsano, having rolled a lump of clay 4–5 kilograms in weight vertically between his palms, adds two or three coils to form one band of the jar. This is pulled up by the master potter as the wheeler turns the wheel. Even though the band already formed may be dry enough to receive the next coil, the weight and pressure exerted make it necessary to bind it with string before the master throws the coil to the required height for the new band, when the string is removed. The separate sections of a large jar – there are usually six – are made visible by the extra coils which are added where two bands join; essential strengthening and decoration are thus combined.

Ladi Kwali applies each coil inside and well below the old rim and draws it up diagonally,

increasing height and diameter as she walks around her pot.

Mallam Garba adds a thick coil of soft clay and dry donkey dung to the scraped and dampened rim of his stiffened pot. First squeezed around and down over the edge with the thumb and forefinger of the right hand, it is squeezed again with both hands as he walks around the pot, thinning and raising the neck. The deep pinch marks, with their diagonal, patterned urgency express the progress of the potter. The whole of the neck and rim have been pinched out of one coil.

This diagonal rhythm is visible in my own pots, where each coil is pinched and squeezed as the pot is turned on the turntable more than once at a moderate and even pace until the thin wall has been extended by about four times the diameter of the original coil.

(Top right) *A coil is added inside and overlapping the rim of a bowl form.*

(Right) *The same coil has been pinched up, heightening and closing the form.*

'Nest' by Elizabeth MacDonald, with coils layered by positional paddling.

Kenneth Beittel lays a hand-squeezed coil of large diameter on the rim of the growing pot and uses an unusual method of bonding, thinning and shaping his pot. Firmly pressing from the inside of the wall against a biscuit-fired stamp held outside, he makes a relatively thin wall whose surface is made up of adjoining hemispherical hollows from the pressing of the fingers, while the outside is textured by the stamp. The wall stretches considerably under the pressure applied, so skill and care are needed to control the form.

This method combines coiling with the paddle and anvil technique. Paddle and anvil are sometimes used in traditional pot making as a substitute for finger bonding. It is a process which bonds, thins and shapes, all at the same time. Another contemporary American potter, Elizabeth MacDonald, uses it for forming and positioning her coils so that they are squashed upon each other. Building up her forms with short, thin coils quickly rolled in her hand, she attaches them very loosely and freely to the ones below, often overlapping them. The joins are made deliberately obvious and the outline of each addition is clear. After each round they are smoothed and scraped from the inside. The outside is paddled to control the form and in such a way that the coils are pushed into each other in layers. Unlike normal coiling a large element of the rhythm of the pot is dependent on the rolling unevenness of the rim; a strong feeling of undulating horizontality is created and emphasised by the quality of the layering.

(Right) *Enlarging a pot by the extended pinch method.*

(Below) *Kenneth R. Beittel adding a coil to his stamped pot 'The Gathering of the Ancients'.*

Adding clay in small units which are pulled up moves away from the inevitable horizontal rhythms of the coil. The method, used in the Kyūshū Province of Japan in the 16th and 17th centuries – perhaps even earlier – is a quick and interesting variant on coiling. A small lump of clay, gently flattened between the hands and pressed to the rim with an overlap of about one third, is pinched up. The object is to keep the thickness of the wall even as it is being extended, and to keep it vertical. Pinching starts

53

Detail of sculpture 'Floating Weave' by Elsbeth S. Woody, built by the extended pinch method, meeting point between pinched pellets visible.

from the centre of each pellet with thumb on the outside and fingers on the inside pinching and moving up equally. As each pat of clay overlaps the one next to it the wall becomes scalloped; each successive row is arranged so that gaps will be filled in. Unlike ordinary coiling the rim is never even; bonding, construction and growth are one and there is a strong vertical movement. When clays of different colour are combined interesting effects can be achieved.

All methods which extend the clay on the pot need considerable skill: one must control the pinching and pulling in such a way that the clay moves up and not out; one has to gain the tactile sensitivity to produce an even wall and to know when to stop to allow the work to harden.

Ewen Henderson's work uses more random additions. He constantly changes his working methods, making use of every possibility in hand-building processes which derive from coiling. He describes his current work as 'assemblages'. Clays which are different in colour, or are coloured by glaze stains or oxides, are sandwiched together and assembled into rough shapes such as crescents and strips. They are placed on the growing pot in such a way that they can be teased and pinched into the final form and pattern. The whole piece is made in a very plastic state and can be worked and changed until it is ready to 'freeze'. The end product often conveys a sense of immediacy, as though the form were balanced at the point of collapse. At the same time it has the timeless appearance of geological age and event working

(Right) *Pot by Ewen Henderson.*

Peter Stoodley refining the form of his pot by beating.

upon material. In Ewen's work bonding, construction, growth, pattern and colour are one.

Shaping

Shaping may or may not be integral to the forming process; the shaping may occur during the layering of the coils, or it may not occur until after the pot has been built. Monica Young, whose pots have a very gently curved silhouette, determines essentially the shape she wants in the way she places her coils. If, subsequently, she needs to alter the curve, she beats from the inside. The shapes of Peter Stoodley's pots are also formed in the building: a final beating is used to clarify, not to change the shape. To build an overhanging vessel on a stem such as his requires a slow and carefully phased operation; he has to wait for the clay to stiffen as the coils are flung out beyond the base. Like many coil builders he works on several pots at the same time. David Roberts also places each coil where he wishes it to be in relation to the clear idea he has of the final form. He uses shaped formers or metal scrapers held against

Maria Martinez scraping the straight-sided, growing pot. Note the gourd scrapers and the traditional, double-spouted wedding pot (c. 1950).

the outside of the wall to control and define it, at the same time whirling his turntable very fast to get a concentric result.

At the other extreme, Maria Martinez left all shaping until the building was completed. Her pots were not very large and were built initially in the form of a cylinder. This allowed her to shape and smooth the inside of the base before pressing outward from inside, forcefully persuading the clay into its final curve. She, too,

Maria Martinez shaping the pot.

had a variety of formers and scrapers to shape and 'clean' the pot: these were made from gourd shells and their different curves would fit a pot of any shape. However, if she were making a large pot which needed to dry a little in the course

57

Beit Shebab potter shaping and enlarging the body, using paddle and anvil.

The coils are carefully laid inside the rim and the form is drawn diagonally inward as Ladi Kwali shapes the neck.

of coiling, some shaping and thinning may have been done while the pot was being built.

The Beit Shebab potters, having coiled a slightly tapering cylinder, beat the clay when it is leather-hard with the paddle and anvil to raise the height, and then beat it again to give the final form as far as the neck join. The strong diagonal strokes give the surface of the jar the appearance of diagonal burnishing.

Ladi Kwali starts her pulled up, modelled form with a slightly flared cylinder which is gradually squeezed, pinched out and scraped until it is ready to receive the coils; these are placed deliberately on the still uneven rim. As she comes to the shoulder near the neck the form is drawn up diagonally inward so that the circumference becomes less. Now, as the rim is nearly reached, more attention is paid to trimming the edge. The flat rim is formed by the final coil.

The rim

Each coil produces a new rim, obliterating the one before it. In this section we use the word

Ladi Kwali using a single coil for the rim, which is widened and moved outward by scraping. Note the importance of the supporting hand.

Mallam Garba shaping the rim, forming it with a curved pod.

'rim' in referring to the way in which the *final* coil finishes the pot.

We have seen that there is a nicety of construction at all stages of the coiling process. This is particularly true as the neck and rim are approached, when the coils must generally be made more carefully, and are rounder and thinner. This is partly because there is often a narrowing at this stage – and the possibility of collapse – and partly because the clay becomes thin as the vessel grows (a vertical cross-section of a hand-built pot – as of one which is wheel thrown – will show thicker clay at the base and gradual thinning as it rises). But most important, it is because the rim – or margin of the vessel

– occupies an important role, and requires a more studied statement.

Ladi Kwali finishes her pot in the traditional, local way, adding a final coil to the outside to form the flat rim. The neck and rim are then rapidly but carefully smoothed with a piece of thin, wet leather held between the fingers while the potter herself moves quickly around the pot. So too the Ibibio potters, sitting and rotating their formers, smooth the neck and rim in much the same way.

Mallam Garba dampens the rim surface, and with the strong, resilient leaf of a bauchi tree folded over it he walks backward around the pot smoothing and strengthening the rim. He then sits to scrape and shape the rotating pot with a curved pod from an African mahogany tree, first the interior and then the outside, at the same time fusing the wet clay to the shoulder.

Gabrielle Koch uses a large, flattened coil to create the rim. The degree of firmness of the main body is critical at this time for the curve of the form has been brought in quite rapidly. The area around the rim must have dried enough to bear the coil and yet still be flexible enough to be formed and luted to it.

The potters of Beit Shebab join together two nearly leather-hard forms – a tall, cylindrical shouldered base and a conical thrown bowl which is dipped into slip and inverted on to the shoulder of the jar. The potter then puts his thumbs through the base and converts it into a neck on the wheel. The forming of these jars combines a multiplicity of techniques – a thrown base enlarged with paddle and anvil, spiral coiling, beating to thin, shaping with paddle and anvil, and finally the addition of a wheel-made shape by throwing, to bond and form.

The rim as the culminating point of the vessel determines much of its dynamic. It mediates between the inside and outside of the pot and defines the point at which they become one; it determines how the vessel relates to the space around it, and at its best it serves to create a sense of inevitability – the conviction that the work is as it is and could be no other way. It may be indeterminate, the wall being carried to the margin of the vessel without a break in the smoothness of the contour, and without a change in thickness: that is, it may follow the general direction of the sides of the vessel. Or it may simply be where the pot finishes (see the pot by Ewen Henderson on p. 55). In making a coiled pot the rim can be at any point where a coil is completed. So this direct rim, simply a part of the growth of the body, will have to be convincingly placed with regard to the proportions of the vessel.

The rim, on the contrary, may be a quite distinct part of the vessel (see the pot by Ladi Kwali on p. 58). It may change direction from the main body of the pot, either sharply or

gradually; it may be thickened or thinned, and it may be elaborated with decoration. In changing direction it may curve gently or abruptly inward or outward, it may rise vertically or depart horizontally from the wall. There may be a neck: then the rim must relate to the spring of the neck. Usually the rim has a clear, taut form but sometimes it escapes this – as in the bowls of the Sepik Province of New Guinea, which at their simplest end with a castellated wall, or the Jōman pots from Japan which are described more fully in the next chapter. If the vessel is functional, too, the rim may have to be modified to satisfy the purpose of the vessel – perhaps for pouring, or for lifting or retaining liquid.

A prehistoric, hand-built jug from Cyprus displays a wonderful unity of form, the rim rising uplifted to the pouring lip and falling

Prehistoric Cypriot earthenware jug, c. 12 cm.

(Left) *Gabrielle Koch carefully placing the flattened coil directly on the rim of her large, partially burnished pot.*

rapidly to the swelling rhythm of the handle. It grows directly from the vessel: if we imagine the right wall continued we can see the necked vessel which has been modified by cutting. It is a jug of great life, elegance and vitality.

Disturbingly balanced and abstractly exciting is the modelled head with rim-forming headdress set asymmetrically on the body of a wine jug from the African Congo.

The rim of a pot made by Elizabeth Fritsch

(Above) *Pot by Elizabeth Fritsch.*

(Right) *Wine jug from the Belgian Congo, Africa. 25 cm.*

flows up into an abstract form reminiscent of a spout, handle or lip. It is indivisibly part of the total form and serves to counterbalance a rocking base, enhancing the airborne appearance of the whole.

Unpredictability of the rim is often a feature in the work of other contemporary potters. Sometimes, as in the work of Elizabeth MacDonald or Ewen Henderson, it is the natural finish, the pot ending irregularly as every coil before it has done. Sometimes the knowledge that the fire acting on the rim of a thin-walled pot will distort it is consciously exploited. Sometimes, as in the work of John Ward, the rim is displaced, but only incidentally, when the whole body is cut and re-formed. Sometimes, as in the deliberate cuts of David Roberts, it is a formally contrived feature. So we see that in some cases the rim describes the making or firing, while in others it is a positive source of embellishment or decoration.

The final shape

The potter can start with a very clear idea of the shape that is to be made and work deliberately towards it. In traditional societies the forms were laid down by convention: to have had to change them would be unacceptable.

But perhaps that coiler, unfettered by convention, starts out with only a generalised idea as to where he is going. He simply uses the clay as it is – wet or dry, stony or fine – and the atmosphere as it is – dry or humid – and has the power within these limitations to pull and push the clay into a satisfying form, each section based on the preceding one, and itself becoming the basis for the section to follow.

Those characteristics of the form which have a bearing on its aesthetic qualities can be analysed: they include proportion, the relation of parts, the form of the curve and the complexity of the contour. In the making, this kind of analysis, essentially verbal, is surely taking place intuitively, in harmony with the material and the intent of the creator. But it is of value, once terms are defined, to assess and make analytical judgements along these lines after the work is completed.

It will be seen, however, that in spite of the infinite possibility of variation, there is a natural form which evolves from the coiling process itself. The method favours rounded, organic curves, full forms that belly out gradually and gently curve into small mouths, spherical shapes that emanate from rounded bases, or walls that grow from flat bottoms and extend to a fulsome richness before they are pulled into the neck. The closed bowl seems to reach a more satisfactory conclusion than the fully opened basin: it is in engineering terms the strongest form and aesthetically one of the most satisfying. Open forms – dishes, plates, wide basins – are difficult to coil.

But because clay can be freely manipulated during the course of building, exaggerated forms can be achieved. For example, the gently curved vessel can be turned into one that squats low and wide before it moves rapidly into the rim.

It may be possible to explain why vessels conform to certain rules of form within a culture, for it may reflect certain rules of form and style of that culture. But what of the universal qualities of shape that have a strong appeal and have been appreciated by different cultures? These cannot be explained by a common canon of forms, and certainly not on the grounds of technique alone. Looking at pots from many areas of the world and from different times one is struck by the amazing similarities that exist between them, and at the same time one marvels at the formidable variety and striking strangeness of so many of them. One sympathises with Dürer who, confronted by the strange works of art of the pre-Columbian Indians wrote: 'Never in all my life have I seen things which thrilled me as much as these objects do. Because I see them as works of a singular art and I was filled with admiration before the subtle ingenuity of men from far-off lands!'

4

Decoration and firing– archaeological and ethnic

In dealing with archaeological and ethnic pots and their decoration we have to remember two important technical points: first, almost all the ware is unglazed; secondly, it is fired to a low temperature that is very unlikely to exceed 1000°C.

What would today be considered disadvantages led to a richness and variety of invention. Clay, by its nature, lends itself supremely to both graphic and plastic techniques. Simple and complex texturing, abstract and figurative painting are all found among the work of early and pre-wheel potters. Embellishments often have no relation to the use of the vessel and it can only be a source of wonder that the creative instinct of man added what was so frequently a purely aesthetic gesture to even the most ordinary and functional of objects.

Generally, the more prestigious the use of the pot, or the occasion of its use, the more elaborately decorated it became. Cooking pots are mainly surface marked, ceremonial vessels more ornate. Among the latter there may be a deep cultural significance in the representation, and the symbols must be correct for the specific ritualistic function of the ceremony – associated perhaps with rain, hunting, or fertility. Sometimes the design may commemorate an

(Left) *Neolithic Yang-shao amphora. 31·7 cm. 2000–1500* B.C.

event or, indeed, it may have the purely decorative value which we see in it now.

The decoration will often have been carried out immediately after the making, and by the maker: in Nigeria it is always done by the makers themselves. Sometimes it will be in the hands of a few proficient craftsmen or women: as we have seen, in Papua New Guinea, women are responsible for the undecorated cooking pots while men make cult objects using decoration as a means of displaying their artistic talent. In other places the women make the pots and the men decorate some of them. The Pueblo potter Maria Martinez made the pots and her husband painted them.

Incidental markings

The most natural decoration is any marking of the surface which arises from – and is intimately related to – the process and the tools which are used in the making.

The simplest of all textures is that made when the surface of a pot is scraped to refine the form, revealing the grog which is dragged across it; as the form is followed there may be a slight directional movement.

The amphora from Neolithic China, made in the Yang-shao culture between 2000 and 1500 B.C., reveals diagonal markings which have been made by beating with a corded paddle; but it is we who enjoy the texture, for the pot was

65

Mogbo Ajayi of Ibibioland, Nigeria, forming a pot by the paddle and anvil process. The coarse cloth stretched to form the anvil is impressed into the clay, leaving its pattern.

probably covered by a slip which has worn away to reveal the stripes and hollows.

The texture which covers the Nigerian pot is made by a cloth draped over the anvil; its pattern is impressed into the clay as the pot is beaten out. It is similar to that found on the Egyptian storage vessel of the 1st or 2nd Century B.C. This was possibly formed by paddle and anvil in a hollow in the ground on which a mat had been laid; the smoother neck is later coiled on. Certainly the delicate patterning, so in keeping with the quiet presence of the pot, appears to have been made in the forming.

Another texture which arises in the making is that produced when a corn cob or gourd rind is rolled over the surface of the pot after the last coil has been laid. This is done on Nigerian cooking pots and is a technique also used by the North American Navajo Indians, among others. It is done partly to even the surface, partly to impact the clay to make it dense and reduce porosity, and partly to roughen the surface to make it easier to handle.

Burnishing

For much the same purpose pots can be burnished or polished, giving the surface a density which will help to seal it. This

(Right) *Egyptian storage vessel decorated with impression of mat and paint. 2nd–1st Century B.C.*

Chinese food vessel with cord-paddled surface. An inscription inside the rim reads: 'made for his father Hsin'. Chinese Chou dynasty.

Early Bronze Age beaker found on a Welsh burial site, impressed decoration. 2500–1500 B.C.

process is also used for decorative purposes: in a way, burnishing is the pre-wheel, pre-kiln equivalent of glaze. The leather-hard clay is rubbed with a hard object, such as a smooth pebble or the back of a spoon, to make it lustrous. The quality of the clay is particularly important: it must be even and smooth to give an all-over lustre. Whether a people made polished pottery or not depended not only on taste and skill but on the kind of clay which was available to them.

Apart from the intrinsic properties of the clay, timing is all-important. The clay must be partly dried and have shrunk enough to retain the sheen, but damp enough to pick one up; if it is too dry the surface remains matt. At the right point the tool, which may be a piece of coconut shell, a large seed or a string of seeds, is worked with considerable pressure as many times as possible over the surface before the clay dries.

The Adarawa potters of Sokoto soak a piece of leather in a thick slip made from the local earth, and wipe it over the lower portion of a water pot in large, sweeping movements as it is revolved in a broken sherd. The pots are dealt with in batches of ten; each layer is allowed to dry before another of several layers is added. The surface is finally polished with a necklace of seeds from the baobab tree. The only part of the pot which is not polished is the bottom, which is left rough so that it can be lifted and held without slipping. The burnishing is carried out by a boy apprentice. In another culture, in a pottery village in Indonesia, it is again children who burnish with round stones the hand-made bowls.

Impressed patterns

Burnishing, carried out at the leather-hard stage, gives a finish to a pot, not a pattern. But the yielding nature of clay in the plastic state allows immediate patterning in a variety of ways, with many possibilities within them.

Patterns pressed into the wet clay were used frequently in very early times, and can be seen on ethnic pots today. Sometimes the surface may be patterned in small units. The range of 'tools' used by the Catawba Indians, for example, is imaginative: it includes objects such as mussel shells, gourd rinds, bamboo knives or stones, and such modern oddments as the looped end of a hairpin, the minted end of a coin, a shoe button-hook or pieces of wire – anything that will make an interesting pattern on the soft clay.

Or, large areas are covered quickly, using cord-wrapped sticks and paddles, or paddles or continuous roulettes bearing carved designs – all methods used in the east of north America.

In the south-east of China, as early as the 8th Century B.C., stamped patterns on the high-fired ware arose first from the process of beating the coiled pots with wooden paddles to improve their shapes. Subsequently the paddles would be carved with designs to stamp the finished vessels with geometric patterns such as trellis, squared spirals or 'stepped line' designs.

In Mexico, pottery stamps were used extensively: they might be flat seals with handles or continuous cylinders. The most elaborate tool used by the Africans is one for decorating the damp clay – the carved wooden or plait-fibred roulette. The Welsh bronze cinerary urn on p. 16 has a variety of impressions arranged in horizontal herring-bone patterns on the inside and outside of the rim and shoulder, a row of oval impressions stamped on the outer band of the rim, and a row of 'horse-shoe' shaped impressions below the upper shoulder.

The beautifully formed and fired early Bronze Age beaker (2500–1500 B.C.) has a punctulated pattern of much richness and order. The clear marks may have been made with the point of a stick or a notched tool, and are likely to have been based on a textile weave. The tools and weapons of this time were of supreme quality, and the design of spear heads, daggers and other artefacts show a sure instinct for form and balance of parts. The same is expressed in this pot, where the balance is subtly enhanced by the distribution of decorated areas and the scale of the design. Such beakers were status symbols recognized over large areas of Europe, and this fine example would have been found in the

tomb of a relatively important man – or, less likely, woman.

Incised patterns

Incised patterns – lines pressed or cut into the clay – can be applied at every stage: the clay may be plastic, leather-hard or even fired. It is a widespread and important technique.

The Ibibio potter, nearly finishing the making of her water jar, uses a tool like a comb to incise four lines where the neck joins the body. This is done while the clay is very soft, and before the rim has been formed.

Ladi Kwali uses the technique for the traditional symbolic images with which she decorates her pots. She draws an outline of the design while the clay is still plastic by incising with a blade – rather like a short pen-knife – made from the hard bark of the raffia tree. She cuts rather than scratches because the clay has a coarse texture: a cut is crisper while scratching

Ikwa Umanah incising the distinctive neck decoration of her region with a comb wrapped in a plantain leaf so that only the tips project.

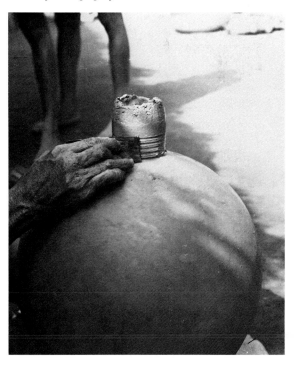

Ladi Kwali: pot with traditional images incised and roulette filled.

would disturb the surface by dragging the grog particles across it. She then uses a roulette to fill in the images she has drawn, first dipping it into water and then gently rolling it with one finger, changing direction with decorative effect.

Two pots from Cyprus show incised lines

Sepik bowl with carved spiral ornament from Papua New Guinea.

drawn in a direct and abstractly decorative way (see p. 28). The decoration of the regularly formed earlier jug is simpler and less assured, following the form in a horizontal plane; that of the more organic double-spouted one is more complex, using horizontal, vertical and diagonal lines to support the bulbous body, and showing confidence in decorative handling. The gypsum-filled incisions make the design stand out from the ground.

Bura pots from Nigeria have red burnished surfaces and incised linear patterns; as we see later, a white slip is occasionally used as an inlay.

Sgraffito

An incision may be so deep that it is more akin to carving. Among many examples of decoration by this method are the deep carvings of symbolic images around the Mayan bowls of pre-Columbian pottery of central America.

Along the Sepik River in Papua New Guinea, burnished conical bowls are deeply incised with curvilinear designs drawn in two parallel lines in the leather-hard stage. The wedge-shaped cutting edge of a tool made from the hard vein of a sago leaf is used to cut between the lines; the clay is removed in chips and long curling ribbons, leaving the pattern engraved into the surface. The bowl is burnished again to smooth the cut edge of the design. The firing – generally done by the women – is in reduction, and turns the pot black; the contrast between the dull track of the carving and the polished upper surface often gives the appearance of carved wood. The craftsmanship in these bowls can be very refined. The vigorously primitive example shown, with typical spiral decoration and strong three-dimensional conical forms has been inlaid or painted along the grooves – a task usually done by the men – with red, yellow, white or black earth pigment taken from a creek and mixed with water.

Applied clay

By adding clay in the form of pellets, coils or slabs, it is possible to create a raised surface

Ikwa Umanah completing the decoration on a large jar; it may be used as a water jar, but the decoration suggests that it will be a musical instrument used in ceremonies. A side hole causes a deep reverberating note to sound when it is beaten by hand.

(Right) *Medieval jug with applied, incised and modelled clay decoration. Ham Green ware, Bristol. 13th Century.*

which manipulates the light and shade even more than texturing or sgraffito.

The Ibibio potter of Nigeria decorating her pot in the leather-hard stage has pressed thin coils of clay in the form of a human or animal figure over her incised design and, using the same comb-like tool which was used to decorate the neck, impresses a decoration on the damp added coil.

Strikingly similar in spirit and technique is the 13th Century Medieval jug from Bristol with its stylised frieze of dancing girls applied in

relief; it too has impressed decoration on the body and legs. The pattern of the circling figures is further enriched by the scratched patterning which follows the spaces around the hand-holding figures. The arm of the girl on the left follows the handle of the jug, and an additional row of heads is modelled on the rim.

Medieval pots – unlike all others described in this chapter – were glazed, for practical rather than decorative purposes. More varied colour was sometimes added by the use of different coloured clays. The 13th Century jug (see p. 18) has triangular areas outlined with dark brown clay and filled in with pellets of light clay and dark brown rosettes.

Medieval pots were at their most elaborate in Britain and Europe between 1250 and 1350 A.D. A jug from that time found in Sussex displays a variety of techniques which exploit the plastic characteristics of clay. There are the impressed finger marks around the base, the applied additions of curved strips on the body, and the moulded form of the rosette and buckle; the head is modelled out of the jug itself. During this period jugs shaped like human beings were popular; as in this one, heads might be modelled as a part of the vessel, the limbs would often be applied in strips of clay.

A historic pot from Benin is highly crenellated and flanged by the addition of strips of clay. Marks impressed by the fingers and in other ways are clearly seen. The form carries with it a richness of organised light and shade that must surely owe something to the courtly art of bronze casting – its fine bronze heads with collared necks and stylised strip-textured hair.

Some of the most extraordinary decorative elaboration to be found arose from the Jōman pottery of Japan, which evolved over a very long period – possibly from as early as 7000 B.C. and continuing until 1000 B.C. In these coiled earthenware pots we see an extreme example of decoration overtaking utility. The word

Flanged, pinched and impressed pot from Benin, Nigeria.

'Jōman', literally translated, means 'cord pattern', and the surfaces of these early pots were invariably thus textured. However, the ornamentation became increasingly sculptural until, characteristically, it eventually became overweight for the size of the vessel. The emphasis is always at the top of the pot; their owners, using them at ground level, would have seen them from above. There are rims that had no smooth surface to drink or pour from, bases too narrow for stability, and decoration too asymmetrical for good balance.

The decoration includes linear relief, slabs of clay joined together, finger-pinched narrow

(Left) *Earthenware jug with moulded decoration under green glaze. Found at Pulborough, Sussex. 32 cm. 14th Century.*

73

ridges, grooves, loops and spirals. The baroque swirls and convolutions result in a great drama of chiaroscuro. It seems that the makers of these pots were striving for maximum artistic effect; in spite of their functional inadequacies it is thought unlikely that any of these pots were purely ornamental – at least until the later Jōman period when some of the vessels would have been used for special and ritual purposes.

It was observed by the noted archaeologist A. V. Kidder that undecorated wares are generally more pleasing in shape than those that bear ornament, particularly appliqué. Yet there is a strange and wonderful freedom in these expressive works which convey an essential mystery we cannot fully share.

Painted pottery

In Africa generally and in Nigeria particularly, the emphasis in decoration is on texture – impressed, incised or added – and colour is rarely used. Occasionally incisions are filled in with colour or, as in the Bakengo pot from the western Congo, a pot may be splashed with vegetable dye when it is hot. Generally, though, light and shade are to act as self colour, often very richly.

The use of coloured earth pigments fired on to the pot is found in early Neolithic pots from other parts of the world. Some of the earliest painted pottery came from west Asia, and the Neolithic pots from Kansu Yang-shao in north-west China evolved from that stimulus in the third millenium B.C. The most striking are the large coiled pots, mainly excavated from burial sites. These are made from fine-grained earthenware which fires to a light red colour. After being lightly burnished to provide a suitable surface they were painted with black, red, maroon and brown designs. The painting was done with a primitive form of brush whose

(Top left) *Middle Jōman beaker, cord-impressed body, elaborately decorated rim. 1500 B.C.*

(Left) *Large pot splashed with vegetable matter from Bakengo, western Congo, Africa.*

Funerary urn, Neolithic Kansu, Yang-shao culture.
35·5 cm. 2000–1500 B.C.

marks can often be seen. The bright red is due
to the pure iron ore haematite, while the black
and maroon are due to varying quantities of iron
and manganese. During the firing the oxides
change in colour from black through to sepia —
variations due to the differing density and
impurities of the pigment.

The repeated patterns are of wide curves of
spirals embellished with serrated edges and
extending in undulating rhythms around the
body of the pot. Only the upper parts of the
large urns would be painted and the patterns are
often bordered, with a broad scalloped band
around the base. While there is a clear identity
of form and patterning among them there is also
a constant variation in detail, as we see by
comparing the pot described on p. 15 with the
one shown here.

These generous, simple forms, with their bold
brushwork and fluency of curvilinear rhythms
are probably the most striking achievements of
the Chinese Neolithic potter.

(Above) *Vases from the Palace of Minos at Knossos, including Melian bird jugs. 2000–1700 B.C.*

(Left) *Decorated vase excavated at Baan Chiang, Thailand. 38 cm. 500 B.C.–500 A.D.*

The vase excavated at Baan Chiang in northeast Thailand is also painted freely. Thousands of such pots, unglazed, with red, geometric and finger-print designs, were recovered from a burial site at Baan Chiang. Thermoluminescence tests date them between 5000 B.C. and 770 A.D. The design on the pot is based on spirals which swell the body – which is not itself rounded – while the area between shoulder and rim is painted with a horizontal flourish, a rhythm which seems to announce the outflung rim.

A group of vases excavated at the beginning of this century from the Palace of Minos at Knossos show that the Minoan civilisation was technically and aesthetically an advanced one. The large pithoi, as we have seen, were decorated in the making with coils and bosses of clay; on other pots the chief characteristic was the painted decoration – white, red, orange, yellow or bluish-black.

In the pots pictured here two – of remarkable regularity and sophistication of form – have the spiral motif painted on them against a dark ground. More commonly the Minoan potter/decorator used subjects from nature: the bold simplification of a flower in brilliant and highly contrasting colours filling the whole of one face – as it does here on the distorted pot lying on its side; the palm tree scratched into a dark panel – on the pot at the far right. The jug and half jug are not Knosson but are typical of the work from Melos: the painting of the birds, wings in flight, echoes the idea of the form – a light and vital movement across the upper half of the pot.

Another splendid example found at Knossos is this heavily reconstructed pot made in the manner of the pithoi. It pictures a curvaceous octopus, its tentacles stretching all over the body of the pot, painted with great vigour and with a sure instinct for the positive and negative of patterning – the representational and the abstract admirably synthesised.

The images of the Minoan were of the natural world around, but they did not include human figures. The polychrome pot, painted in red, black and purple on a buff body from the province of Veraguas in Panama (1000–1500 A.D.) represented a god figure in the kind of stylised way that would be found in other art forms – in relief decoration on buildings, in carvings and wall paintings; the images were a part of the mythology of the culture. The geometry of the rhythms and swirls are symbolic and represent the crocodile god. The satisfying refinement of the form is complemented by the positioning of the semi-abstract figure which is both angular and

(Top right) *Octopus-painted jar found at Knossos, made in the same way as the pithoi, with coils of clay thrown on. 13th Century* B.C.

(Right) *Crocodile god bowl, Veraguas, Panama. 24·8 cm. 1000–1500* A.D.

curved, and which follows, and is contained by, the horizontal parallel lines.

Slip

Slip, as we have seen, can be used to give a smooth texture to a coarse body for burnishing, but it also introduces the possibility of colour as well as providing a smooth ground on which to paint.

A mixture of clay and water, it is usually of a finer and richer clay than that of the body it is to cover, and may also be of a different colour. It must adhere well to the body, neither peeling nor crazing, must have good covering power, and must fire to the same temperature as the body. It is always applied to a moist clay.

By coating a pot with a slip of a different colour and incising or cutting through to the ground, we can produce a particoloured pot. The Mexicans used this method with formalised and hieroglyphic designs.

Alternatively, it is possible to inlay slip of a different colour into an incised or impressed surface. By painting over the relief pattern while the clay is damp, and scraping off the excess slip when it has almost dried, a crisp colour contrast can be attained. It was a technique used widely in Cyprus about 2000 B.C., and is sometimes used in Bura in Nigeria and in Papua New Guinea now.

Complex and elaborate designs can be painted with coloured slips: some of the best known are those of the Pueblo potters of Arizona and New Mexico. The isolation and cultural conservation of the villages, many retaining their own languages, meant that pottery from each pueblo retained its own distinctive style. About ten pueblos are still making pottery (no longer for domestic and ritual use but for the commercial market) and it was due to two women, who became well-known, that the two-thousand-year-old, dying craft was revived. They were the Hopi Indian Lesse Nampeyo, and Maria Martinez from San Ildefonso on the Rio Grande valley, both from the Tewa tribe. Their separate attempts to emulate the pottery of the past were precipitated by local archaeological excavations.

Nampeyo was the wife of one of the men working on a site in 1895 and revived the pre-Columbian ware of Sikyatki from pot sherds found there. Through experiment and skill she developed the shapes and decorations into her own style. The old Sikyatki pots were wide-shouldered and squat, with direct rims, and Nampeyo has exaggerated this tendency.

Martinez's pots would, like all Pueblo pottery, be given a base coat of slip applied in a similar way to the Sokoto (Africa) method. Fine clays without opener are soaked in water until they are smooth, with the consistency of cream; they are then applied to the pot with a cloth in 4–6 layers, each layer being applied to a dry surface. Before the final layer is dry the pot is polished with a smooth water-worn pebble.

The Hano clay, which Nampeyo had to find to match the original pots, is light in colour, turning in firing from yellow to a warm ivory buff. Slips ranging from ochre, light yellow, orange-red to red-brown and black are made from a vegetable dye mixed with iron. The brush is made from narrow slivers of yucca, 15–30 centimetres long, chewed until the fibres are separated to form a very fine point capable of painting very fine detail. Areas to be painted are marked off with a finger nail or charcoal. The short brush is held between thumb and forefinger while the rest of the hand rests on the pot to keep it steady. Religious motifs – rain clouds, water serpents, eagles' feathers, bear paws, lightning, deer – were once used for their magic associations. The designs of Nampeyo and Martinez have incorporated the same symbols but used them in an abstract way. The scenes are no longer part of the cultural and religious life.

In the pot illustrated Nampeyo has decorated the traditional area, from the flat top to below the shoulder, aware of the curvature and unity of the pot. The scrolls are typical of the tradition but have departed from it, no longer denoting the sun, the earth, the moon and sky. The buff base colour is also incorporated positively to add a third colour to the red and ochre pattern. The division into small geometric units ensures that

Slip-painted pot by Lesse Nampeyo, Pueblo Hopi, Arizona. Yellow ware with red and black painted decoration. 16 cm high, 34 cm diameter.

any part of the design in the field of vision is of interest.

Nampeyo, who died in 1942, greatly stimulated but also radically changed the craft, which is still being practised by her great grand-daughter as well as by others.

Maria Martinez made the polychrome pots of her pueblo as a young girl, using the traditional technique, and continued to make them in collaboration with her husband Julian until his death in 1943. But long before this she had been asked to make samples in a style known only through black, glossy sherds found in archaeological excavations near San Ildefonso. She was able to reconstruct the old forms, and to polish their surfaces to give the deep sheen

characteristic of the local aesthetic, but could not at first make them black. Finally, Julian succeeded in producing a carbonised body by smothering the flames of the bonfire with dry dung and wood ash half an hour before the end of firing. This reduced atmosphere caused the iron-rich slip to become black. The first blackware pottery was probably made in 1910, and in the following thirty years the pots became blacker, thinner, more glossy and more symmetrical. Julian, the decorator, improved his procedures too. As they become better known these Pueblo potters – for the first time – had their signatures attached to their work.

An innovation introduced by the Martinez team, which has no historical precedent in the region, was the use of black on black. The highly burnished pot is decorated with a further slip which will remain matt during firing, leading to a striking and sophisticated play between lustrous image and dull, black ground.

79

Black on black jar made by Maria Martinez, decorated by Julian Martinez. San Ildefonso Pueblo (1920).

The decoration by Julian of the single curve of the water serpent winding around the pot has an austerity belied by the richness of the blacks.

Black lustre on matt black is also used as a decoration in Ilorin in Africa. Here only the pattern, not the whole vessel, is burnished. The pot is carbonised by being put into a heap of wet leaves, then dipped into a liquor made from the locust bean pod, which seals the carbon into the pores.

Firing processes

Much of the pottery that has been described here has been fired, essentially, in the open. In these open firings the most simple means and materials have produced very efficient firing techniques compatible with the conditions and the uses to which the vessels were to be put. For the primitive kiln is no more than a bed of leaves, palm fronds or dung on which the pots are laid, covered with sherds and heaped with more fuel. When it is set alight, firing is very rapid indeed.

The Ibibio women, illustrated here, lay palm fronds in a criss-cross way then arrange their pots, the first layer on a tripod of briquettes made from decayed house wall mud and sherds, and the rest, rim downward, building a pyramid-like mound which is covered with more palm fronds. In this firing there were 24 pots – small water-carrying vessels used by children, and food bowls. The archaeologist Keith Nicklin observed that the first pot was removed from the fire after 18 minutes and the last after 23 minutes; in that brief time a temperature of 940°C had been reached. This is an example of a particularly quick firing but other records confirm the surprising speed of such firings, which rarely take as long as two hours. In Papua the firing time is usually about half an hour, and the temperature reached between 700° and 900°C. In Namibia recorded times varied between 49 and 85 minutes.

The rise in temperature is particularly rapid in the initial stages, quickly reaching 500–600°C – the point of ceramic change where the body becomes usefully hard and after which plasticity cannot be regained. We have mentioned the importance of openers, which limit the stress caused by the sudden rise in temperature. All the pots in the Ibibio firing illustrated were, indeed, complete and saleable.

Other potters, from many parts of Africa and from Papua, for example, pre-heat their pots by burning fronds or dry grass inside them, or by inverting them over a fire and heating them until they are bone dry.

Michael Cardew, in his pioneering studies of firing methods in Gwari, maintains that the techniques are based upon a 'profound if unconscious knowledge of the scientific principles involved'.

Sometimes the open firing is carried out in a more or less permanent structure – in fact, a <u>primitive kiln.</u> The Hopi Indians fire with sheep dung, and in order to prevent burn marks the pots are protected by large sherds which, in effect – and quite incidentally – form a rudimentary kiln.

Wurno, 27 miles north of Sokoto in northern Nigeria, is an area where flagons are produced in enormous numbers. The firing areas show the typical grate with the walls blackened at the fire holes, or air vents. The grates are made of clay, dung, straw, stones and broken pottery fragments reinforced with local rope, and are simply circular walls about a metre high and four to five metres in diameter, with fire holes every few feet.

The pots are packed soon after sunset by a 'master' – who has the pots handed to him as he stands inside the wall – in such a way that air and flames can circulate freely around them. Great care is taken to support the first, sparse

Ibibio women and a small firing of pots.

Firing area of the men's pottery at Wurno, Nigeria, producing Sokoto flagons. Note typical firing grates with air vents at their base, and burnished ware stacked in the background.

A partly loaded kiln, Thrapsano, Crete (1981).

layer with sherds, packed at various angles; the packing becomes denser and the gaps decrease as the mound is carried up above the wall to a height of a few metres. It is covered with old sherds, then with dry grass, wood or cow dung. Long corn stalks or bamboo are fed into the eight fire holes as the fuel, and firing is completed in an hour or two. The temperature is not nearly uniform, but in some parts may be as high as 850°C. It is a commercial industry; the pots are unpacked by the men and boys, graded and priced by the women and taken to market at once.

In many societies a hole is cut in the ground, or a section cut into a bank to form a pit kiln. The firings take longer, and the cooling process is correspondingly longer, but higher temperatures are reached because the heat is better conserved.

In Ancient Egypt there is evidence of shallow pit kilns where the pots in the firing chamber were separated from the hearth and chimney.

The Yang-shao pottery of Neolithic China was fired in a simple kiln chamber cut into the ground, with the fire to one side and lower than the shelf on which the wares were placed. A number of holes in the shelf allowed passage of the flame; over the top a dome with a central

flue was lightly constructed, and probably rebuilt for each firing. As in the Cretan kilns described below the pots were partly separated from direct contact with the fire. Temperatures of 900°C–1020°C were normal, though higher temperatures could be reached. The surprisingly early appearance of the relatively high-fired ash glazes on hand-built pots during the Shang dynasty (1300–1028 B.C.) can be attributed partly to their advanced firing procedures and kiln design. High-fired ash glazes seem to have been the first to be developed in China; in west Asia and Europe they were not produced until the 18th Century.

In an account of firing in Thrapsano, in Crete, today (see Bibliography), the vertical kiln is described as an upright cylinder built largely below the ground. The fire box is separated from the chamber – where the pots are stacked – by a floor, in which there are small openings. The top of the kiln is covered with galvanised iron sheets (probably pieces of broken pottery in Minoan times) lying on the wall, and the pots are placed loosely so that smoke can escape. It is an 'up-draught' kiln, and elaborately built. Wood is fed in a controlled way through the stoke hole and the burning embers are moved around with a fork. A temperature of about 900°C is reached; the time taken in a firing depends on the size of the kiln and the density of packing.

Medieval potters also used pit kilns, lined with clay or stone. They would have been open

Drawing of the upright kiln used in Thrapsano, Crete.

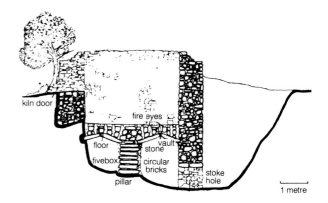

at the top and covered with peat or turves laid on a tile base and bonded with clay; the fuel would be wood, coal or peat. Excavations have shown a wide variation of shape and structure in these kilns and there is evidence of additions being made progressively to their linings in some cases, and of the number and position of the flues being changed – presumably to improve the performance.

The vertical kiln is the oldest of all and was developed from the open-hearth method of firing. The Beit Shebab potters use a modified <u>horizontal kiln</u> having a vertical chimney. Horizontal kilns are known from remains found along the west coast of Europe, from the Mediterranean to the Hebrides, and date from between 2000 and 1000 B.C.; they have been used continuously in China. They are more efficient than the vertical kiln because the horizontal flue spreads the heat and gases more evenly through the kiln and allows the draught to be controlled more easily.

In the Beit Shebab kiln a step is cut out of the hillside to give a flow of heat in both the vertical and horizontal directions. There are two firing chambers, the upper level taking most of the load; the lower level is filled to one third its capacity and a large space is left clear for firing and for the upward passage of smoke and heat. Up to 7000 kilograms of wood of any sort is used

Cut-away drawing of a kiln at Beit Shebab showing loading of the upper level through the main loading door and the lower level through the firing door.

in the firing; the maximum temperature reached is about 800°C. Firing such a load – there might be 1500 pots of different shapes and sizes fired at one time – takes eight days and is usually carried out three times a season.

Post-firing procedures

In some cases porosity may be desirable, particularly in water jars in hot countries, where the slow seepage helps to keep the liquid cool. In other cases the inevitable porosity of low-fired ware has to be overcome. We have seen that burnishing before firing seals the pores as well as achieving a shine, but many low-fired pots are given post-firing treatments to achieve the same end. It is done while the pots are still hot, immediately after they are drawn from the kiln.

Some Nigerian potters rub a bunch of green leaves around the rim and neck of the pot to give a purple stain, while the rest of the surface is rubbed with resin. Yoruba potters soak and boil a number of tree barks and pods and paint or sprinkle the solution on the red-hot pots, to give the desired effect – a fresh, shiny brown surface. Some south-west American Indians boil desert plants to make a liquid which, smeared over their pots, soaks into the pores and makes them water-tight.

The result of applying a lacquer-like substance after firing is found on certain classic Mayan ware. Cretan pots are first rinsed, then filled with water and left to stand for at least a month; the walls gradually become impermeable and suitable for storing oil. Fijian pots are decorated with vegetable dye or daubed with pitch straight from firing. In Cyprus large storage jars for wine, still hot from the fire, are coated inside with resin, or sometimes cement, to make them impermeable.

The balance between the practical and the aesthetic is differently weighted in each case. Sometimes the decorative quality is more or less incidental, and sometimes it is deliberate. The same ambivalence of emphasis is found throughout the process of pot building, and later in the uses of glaze.

5

Contemporary potters and their decoration

The contemporary potter is armed with explicit technical information about clay and its behaviour, about firing methods, pigments and colouring agents, and can consciously select what, how and why he makes. If he is a hand-builder he has already rejected the totally utilitarian, the duplication of a 'production run' and the necessity of speedy making – the wheel provides all these. So what does he make, and how does he decorate it?

Decoration is not a word that many contemporary potters would use to describe the textures and surfaces they give to their work, because it suggests a separation between form and patterning. However, I shall use the term, as I have in the previous chapter, to describe any mark or colour appearing on the surface which enhances the pot.

I shall take examples of the work of some contemporary potters who use the coiling method, to illustrate the way in which they have used the decorative techniques of their predecessors, and other treatments which belong particularly to themselves. There are open to them the extra opportunities given by high-temperature firings and the use of glazes, both rich in creative potential. The science of firing and the chemistry of glazes are, of course, used in all forms of ceramics and will be dealt

(Left) David Roberts: Coil built vessel, raku fired. 30·5 cm.

with here incidentally and only as they relate to individual works. Suffice it to say of firing that the difference between a bonfire, an earthenware and a stoneware firing is mainly one of temperature; suffice it to say of glaze that it is applied to the pot as a creamy liquid by dipping, pouring, spraying or painting – the thickness of the cream depending on how it is to be applied and what result is intended – and that the powdered ingredients can be bought, either ready mixed, or to be mixed by the potter to his own recipes.

Incidental markings

The direct relationship between texture and form is more evident in coiling than in other methods of making pots. We have already seen in Chapter 3 that there are potters whose process is such that surface interest and form are one.

This is at its most unobtrusive in the work of Monica Young, whose unglazed pots have a pleasant, granulated surface and the colour of dark toast. The texturing occurs in the scraping, carried out with a flexible length of 'Surform' blade. When the pot is dry it is sandpapered expressly to roughen the surface further, chalk is rubbed into the pot to darken the colour and it may then be sanded again. The reduced firing, to the high temperature of 1300°C, also adds to the unaccented colour interest. Because of the

John Ward: stoneware bowl, oxide inlaid (1983).

Elizabeth MacDonald: stoneware pots. c. 25 cm.

Ewen Henderson: stoneware pot.

scale and the simplicity of these very large pots, each feature – the top of a smooth rim, a scored line around it, a petal-like overlap, a bevelled base – creates a strong pattern of light and shade.

The integration of form and surface is often a self-conscious preoccupation of potters today, who may deliberately emphasise incidental markings which arise naturally. One way of doing this is by painting oxide, coloured slip or glaze into the body and scraping it off, so that the hollows, dents, scrape marks or finger dimples become coloured. John Ward applies a thin wash of copper manganese and china clay to his bowls and then wipes it off.

Elizabeth MacDonald highlights the texture of her pots by brushing diluted glaze on the outside, and rubbing it off so that it remains only in the indentations; the inside is generally glazed and the work is fired in an electric kiln to a stoneware temperature.

Ewen Henderson expresses his conviction of the oneness of form and decoration even more deliberately. Decoration is structural, and the units for structuring are clays of different bodies or clays mixed with stains and oxides; the variegated colour and the marks made in the forming are incorporated into the finished surface texture of the pots, which are fired to a

(Left) *Monica Young: reduced stoneware pots. c. 150 cm.*

Gabrielle Koch: burnished earthenware pot, sawdust smoked. 39 cm.

stoneware temperature. Sometimes the pots are raw glazed, a technique in which the glaze is applied to the unfired pot. The accidents of any glazing process – 'blobbing', crawling, running – are accommodated in his pots which are often patchy, marbled, or striated. They reveal the influences of the sea, the landscape and found objects on his work, which he says refers also to many cultures, particularly those of the eastern Mediterranean – the Cycladic, early Greece and Cyprus.

Burnishing

In our society pots are burnished for aesthetic reasons only. For Gabrielle Koch who is stirred by the elemental nature of pottery, it is a direct and simple way of working the surface. Her burnished pots, which are sometimes first

dipped into either a red slip or one coloured with oxides, are fired to 900°C and then smoked in sawdust, causing the pots to become partly carbonised. She sometimes raku fires her pots: after a biscuit firing to 900°C in an electric kiln she may glaze sparsely and fire in a reduced atmosphere to 900°C in a gas kiln, withdrawing the pot while it is still glowing hot and smothering it in sawdust for 10–15 minutes. There is a fuller description of a raku firing in the discussion of the work of David Roberts.

The pot illustrated shows the effects of the elements: it has taken on a new form under the pressure of the fire, and the sheen of the burnishing – the marks of the process clearly visible – has been deadened by the heat of the sawdust while the smoke produced by it has created its own patina.

Magdalene Odundo also dips her pots in slip before burnishing them; in fact, layers of clay

Magdalene Odundo: black pot with angled top. 35 cm.

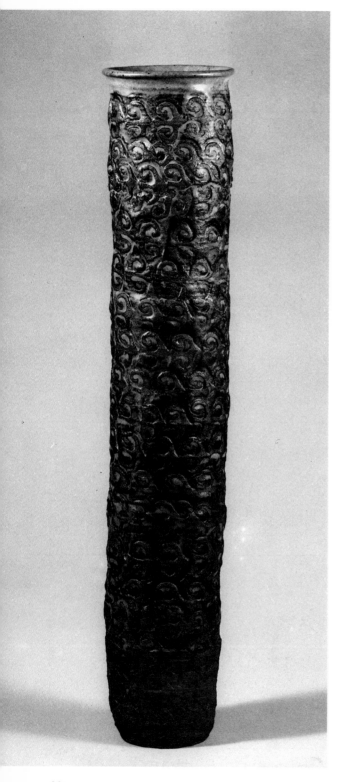

slip are painstakingly polished before firing. Although the body is a red terra-cotta colour it sometimes becomes rich black in a second reduction firing. The work is fired between 900° and 1080°C with a second firing between 700° and 800° for the black ware.

Because her round-bottomed pots are traditionally coiled, and smoothed by sections of shaped gourd rind, they have a strong affinity with traditional forms; however, there are clear indicators to show that this is actually sophisticated and original contemporary work. There is often a strangeness of balance, an asymmetry – at the neck in particular – a tilting of the rim and an austerity of decoration, of incised and applied lines, which belong to each form uniquely.

Impressed patterns

The method used by Kenneth Beittel, with a seal as anvil, has already been described in Chapter 3. Here, too, forming and decorating are one. The impress is made with the tool which thins and stretches the wall as it is pressed into the plastic coil of the clay. The pressure of the stamp causes an irregularity which gives dynamic quality to this tall cylindrical form, while the patterning creates a richness of organised texture. The slight meanders of tension in the column are finalised crisply by a thrown rim on the black stoneware, ash-glazed 'Tall cylinder'.

Incised patterns

Peter Stoodley builds garden pots which he incises with a hacksaw blade. He tries to make the decoration 'enlarge upon and assist in defining shape'. With a large, flat brush he paints a vitreous slip, either black or white, over the major part of the pot, and scrapes it off when it is leather-hard. The slip remains in the incised rhythms and in any fingering made in the forming.

(Left) *Kenneth R. Beittel: 'The Tall Cylinder'. 55·8 cm.*

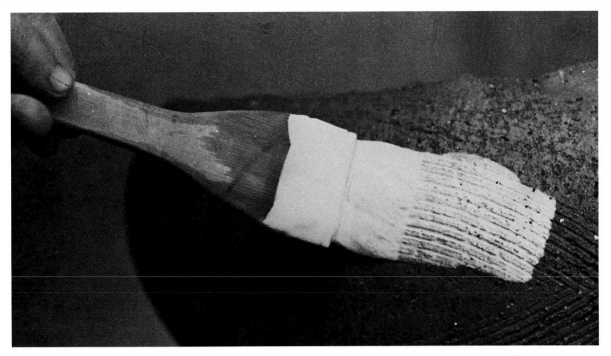

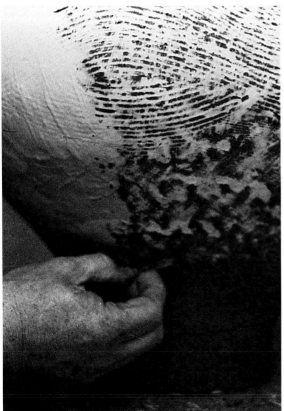

(Above) *Peter Stoodley painting slip on his stemmed pot.*

(Left) *Peter Stoodley scraping away the slip, which remains inlaid in the incised pattern and any marks below the top surface.*

(Below) *Peter Stoodley: finished garden pot.*

Siddig EL'nigoumi builds his pots from a buff clay which he coats in a red or black slip; he brushes it on, using a good, soft brush which will not shed hairs. At the right moment, when the slip is nearly dry, he burnishes the pot. Sometimes he dangles it from a stick over a small pile of burning newspapers to smoke it, then returns the shine with a light polish of beeswax; or he may engrave it immediately after burnishing, before the slip has completely dried.

The pot illustrated has a red slip, and the formality of the crisply engraved pattern may owe something to his interest in textiles. While he is also deeply interested in the artefacts and architecture of his own country, the Sudan, he may use symbols commonly seen about him in England – the CND, British Rail or Underground signs, for example – as abstract patterns, totally detached from their context.

Sgraffito

This thin-walled pot by Judy Trim is made from a coarse, white, rather non-plastic reinforced clay called 'T material'. The austere white of the unglazed body bears the indentations of the coiling process, shown by a gentle ripple of light and shade on the full body. The neck, more finely scraped, has a stony appearance appropriate to the precise nature of the carved decoration, which is a pleated pattern of light and shade contained in a triangle carved from the main body; this fans out to the rim and gently repeats the flare of the narrow-based neck. The inside of the neck contains no incident, and is smoothed by burnishing.

A coiled stoneware vase by Helen Pincombe has been dipped in a dark slip and, rather like the Mexican pots treated in this way, has a formal pattern made of counter-changed units occupying the upper part of the pot cut through to the light clay body, so that there is a strikingly positive pale design on a dark ground.

(Left) *Burnished and incised pot by Siddig EL'nigoumi.*

Judy Trim: stoneware pot (1982).

Helen Pincombe: coiled stoneware vase, sgraffito decorated (1958).

93

Ruth Duckworth: coiled stoneware pot. 19·5 cm (1960).

In subtle contrast is Ruth Duckworth's pot made with a similar technique. The footed form has been dipped in black slip over which a blue matt glaze has been applied. The decoration has been cut through the glaze in a free linear way, following horizontally the main characteristic of its form – its width. The informal decoration covers the pot from foot to shoulder and the blue/black contrast is muted, the random pattern secondary to the form.

Resist and raku

Although the quality of David Roberts' work owes much to his method of firing, it has a precision of building, a thinness of wall and a controlled sophistication of decoration which is not usually associated with the technique of raku. The pots are first biscuit-fired in an electric kiln to 950°C, then sprayed with combinations of underglaze stain, slips and glazes – one piece sometimes fired three or four times in the oxidising atmosphere. The decoration used in preparation for the raku firing uses the 'resist' technique in which masking tape forms stripes across the body to the rim, sometimes both inside and outside the pot before the final, thin coat of raku glaze is sprayed over the pot. The masking tape is removed and the pot left for as long as twenty-four hours to make sure that it is thoroughly dried. The decorative effect of the carbon-inlaid crazing is one of the results of the processes employed in the raku firing, for which he uses a simple kiln formed from an oil drum cut in half and insulated with ceramic fibre, heated by a gas poker.

(Right) *David Roberts: coiled vessel, raku fired. 45 cm.*

Sara Radstone: stoneware pot. c. 50 cm (1983).

The pot – for these are large pieces and are fired singly – is placed on a fire brick and the kiln is warmed up, at first gently. The pressure of the burner is increased gradually until the temperature reaches the melting point of the glaze. The moment at which he knows the glaze will be mature is judged by the colour of the fire, estimated to reach a temperature between 950° and 1050°C. The total firing takes about 45 minutes. The pot is removed red hot, wonderfully molten, flowing and glowing, and left in the air to set. Water is splashed on it to produce the crazing in a controlled way; quite quickly the pot is placed in a bin filled with fine, dense sawdust so that it is smothered for the post-firing reduction. This causes the pot to carbonize; the black soot formed can be brushed from the glazed area but will remain in the lines of crazing.

The black-on-black decoration, although achieved in a different way, shows – as in the pot of Maria and Julian Martinez – the richness of the shiny against the matt. Here the glazed lines move diagonally from the cut of the rim, wrap around the body, setting up a tension with the outer form and then, reappearing on the inside, create a tension between the inner volume and outer silhouette.

Building up, incising and painting

Sara Radstone makes fragile, thin-walled forms which appear at the same time relaxed and nervous. Her way of making them also appears very relaxed. From a pinched ball of clay she adds coils which are bonded in blocks; at this stage the growth is very irregular, quick and casual, for although the shape is beaten with a wooden spoon to consolidate and thin it, none of the usual concern for form is apparent. It is as though she is building herself an enclosed canvas on which to work. Now she builds up patches with extra clay and enhances hollows to create a dented, knobbly surface, further disturbed by the incision of squares which create the effect of a grid. Although these are random, they sometimes pick out the bumps and cavities, and are sometimes painted with bright slips or oxides. After the biscuit firing the glaze is brushed on and scored through, adding to the grid, which follows the body of some of her pieces. The nervous quality lies in the rim, which not only defines the thinness of the wall but also its delicate vulnerability, and in the grid lines, which look like a sagged barbed-wire fence struggling to climb and contain the slumping form.

She deliberately patinates the surface with incidental marks, with 'accidents' created on purpose. The method of making has not created the marks: rather has the imprint of urban deterioration in part created the method. In the same way the idea of the crumpled objects of instant obsolescence – the squashed, discarded beer can, the crushed fender of a car – has inspired the form. Her influences are such things as the tattered accumulation of posters

found on site hoardings or the interiors of
partially demolished buildings, the rusting,
discarded surfaces found in the centre of a city.

Painting

Nearly all John Ward's work is based on the
bowl or upon variants of that form. In limiting
his subject area he has found many ways to
exploit it. The scale of his work ranges from
large bowls of great refinement and strength to
smaller and more vase-like forms: each has a
rightness of scale and proportion. Many of his
ideas have come from experiments with the
cutting and rejoining of forms; grooves and
ridges formed in this way divide and remake the
swelling curves of the pot. Painted bands
emphasise the channel caught between the
rounded fullnesses of the pot. The influence of
decoration upon form creates an illusion of
movement but any optical effect is very gentle
and the lines are, rather, reminiscent of the
furrow of a plough tracing the folds of the
downs as it follows them. He recognises that his
pots are close to many natural forms but does
not draw on any directly.

He relies on three glazes, all of them matt: a
white and a black, which he sprays on, and a
brown, breaking to blue, which is poured.
Beneath the white glaze he uses mixtures of
copper carbonate, lithium carbonate, titanium
oxide and china clay. The pots are oxidised
stoneware and are glaze-fired to a temperature
of 1250°C.

In my own coiled forms the tension of the
silhouette, the sense of a continuous sheet of
clay welded together by pinching, and the
consequent defiance of gravity by scale and
fragility, are important features; so is the
wholeness of the volume contained in that form.
A translation of form by the effects of fire – the
work is glaze-fired to 1260°C – is encouraged by
the thinness of the pot relative to its scale and
by the fact that it is built to the maximum width
of the kiln. In the firing the circular rim, the
upper body and, indeed, the whole proportion
will be re-created as the desired warping occurs.

The surface decoration redefines both the

John Ward: stoneware bowl. 1983.

*Betty Blandino: stoneware pot. 44 cm high, 33·5 cm
wide (1983).*

Gordon Baldwin: 'Grey painting in the form of a bowl', earthenware (1982).

way of making – the scratches and pressures of the fingers and thumbs – and the tautness of the form; often a freely brushed informal movement across the whole form does this. In this vessel a formal design of copper manganese oxides and powdered clay has been painted freehand, the brush having the width of each line, and then scraped off. The image recedes into the surface, like a worn fresco or a painted exterior wall pitted by time; the scraping also reveals the patterning of the building process. The clay is lightly speckled, a mixture of St Thomas white and an ironstone body. The pot is tin-glazed by pouring inside and spraying, thinly, outside.

Gordon Baldwin has been described as an artist who uses some of the materials and techniques associated with pottery. This is not the place to describe the variety of techniques and ideas that inform his largely sculptural work; we shall consider one example that will suit the purpose of this book. Unlike the painted pots we have looked at so far, his coiled bowl forms are essentially vehicles for painting – an intention implicit in the title of this one: 'Grey painting in the form of a bowl'.

The earthenware form is made of extruded coils, and is then beaten wafer thin. The dry, highly reflective white surface is particularly opaque and rich, because it is built up layer upon layer of thin white slip, with kiln firings between applications. The process of repainting and refiring to achieve the effect he wants means that it may take as long as six months to complete a pot. He speaks of having to find the affinity between the real and the implied image of such a bowl and, indeed, the surface itself has an apparent depth so that the painted image appears sometimes submerged below it, sometimes slowly rising to its top, sometimes clearly on and sometimes floating above it. In fact, the final drawings and paintings result from drawing and painting under, in or on top of the slip layers. He uses bistre crayon or oxides, often painted into incised lines.

The paintings – hushed, minimal, smudged, 'rubbed out' – wander around the whole form. The interior no more receives them than does the fluid rim, or the flange upon it, or the exterior. The source material and influences for Baldwin's work are wide-ranging: they include the sculpture of Jean Arp, the paintings of Nancy Baldwin, the writings of John Cage, music and the work of Stockhausen, landscape, 'order on the verge of chaos' and 'a desire for poetry to happen'.

Slip painting

Elizabeth Fritsch too makes painterly pots, but very different in mood and concept from those of Gordon Baldwin. Her coil-built stoneware pots are painted with slips coloured by mixtures of various metal oxides or with glaze stains. They are painted precisely with a semi-matt finish and often in brilliant colours, which are close-toned but distinct.

Others of her pots play a double game, form and surface each creating its own illusions. She has made 'optical' cups, jugs and bottles; for example, one mug has been flattened until it is almost a bas-relief with an elliptical rim that a normal round-sectioned vessel would only *appear* to have in perspective as one looked across it. On top of this is painted a cube in

Elizabeth Fritsch: reduced stoneware pots, slip decorated.

Betty Blandino: double pot, earthenware, 60 cm (1975).

Mary Rogers: 'Triple Slide', stoneware.

perspective, the wall of the mug becoming the apparent far wall of the cube. The resulting painted form is very like a cup painted by Ben Nicholson, with its dry, close-toned quality.

Yet others of her pots, like the larger one on p. 99, make use of sophisticated geometric designs painted in one or two systems intertwined across them, producing a mesh of graduated pattern that creates a harmonious rhythm with the vessel but distinct from it, as the superimposed designs displace the spatial certainty on the surface.

We have seen, in the wine jug from the African Congo and a pot by Elizabeth Fritsch, on p. 62, how the rim of the pot can create a new form as it extends the space of an essentially simple shape.

The pot illustrated here stretches even further into space as a new pot grows out of the rim of another, creating areas of light and shade and a serpentine silhouette. The burnishing of the unglazed surface makes use of the decorative qualities of the clearly visible pinched coils.

Mary Rogers' pot, 'Triple Slide', is a form moving asymmetrically sideways into space. The title is ambiguous, suggesting that the minor forms are sliding down the main body, but also that the lower lip and container are there to collect an overflow from the notched rims above them. Indeed, she says that the idea of water passing over the flat, stone shelf of her own garden waterfall is somehow embedded in it. In spite of this romantic notion the pot is essentially architectural in conception and realisation.

The versatility of coiling is well illustrated in this pot, built on a pinched base, all three forms emerging by pinching from the initial lump of clay. Coiling was begun immediately the third curve had been formed. Finally, the triple form was re-balanced, and an upright, stable image achieved, by scraping and adding clay.

The crawled surface is the result of the carefully monitored interaction between a matt white glaze and a dark, blue-black slip: as soon as the glaze bubbles the kiln is turned off.

Elsbeth S. Woody: 'Floating Weave' reduced stoneware unglazed installation. 250 cm square by 45 cm high (1980). See detail on p. 54.

So far in this book we have considered single works, all of them vessels, pots or containing forms. I shall finish with an example which is none of these and uses the potential of hand-building techniques for creating large-scale works. It comes from an American potter, Elsbeth Woody, who makes environmental pieces – units which are combined to form an architectural presence. She works in multiples of simple, abstract units which she is able to fire separately in her kiln; with them she can make large installations. Because the individual unit is kept very simple it is the interaction between several of them which creates the form. In 'Floating Weave' the strands are built as a unit – like the one to be seen in the background of the photograph – which is then cut into three sections for firing. Each strand was started at the

contact points with the floor and built up by the extended pinch method described in Chapter 3. Although a template was used as a guide there is a slight variation among them which adds an organic feeling to the whole.

The advantages of using the unit method of construction are twofold: there need be no limit to the scale of the work, and its form can be changed with each installation. This is particularly true with units which are even simpler: for example, one installation, 'Grove', is a series of seven columns, each made up of four cylindrical drum-like shapes placed upon each other, reaching to a height of about 3 metres. The relation of each column to the others, to the space around it and to the light source can be varied each time the piece is set up; the viewer's perception of space is manipulated both by the placing and by his own movement in and around it. There is no colour in these abstract forms, fired to around 1180°C and usually in reduction – as in 'Floating Weave'.

6

Contemporary hand-building in context

So far the work of contemporary potters who use the technique of coiling has been viewed through their methods of making and decorating. Let us, finally, attempt briefly to place it in the context of pottery as a whole in Britain in this century; because the idea that coiling might be considered seriously as a contemporary technique, outside tradition, and as a vehicle for self-expression, is relatively new, and it is worth asking how it arose.

This cannot be done without discovering that the notion of the *artist-craftsman* is itself surprisingly recent. At the beginning of this century artist and craftsman occupied distinct rôles. An artist who worked in the pottery industry would design on paper the form and decoration which were to be executed by professional throwers and decorators. There were a few artists, such as Bernard Moore (1850–1935) and William Moorcroft (1872–1945), who decorated pots thrown for them. And there were still 'country potters', artisans serving their own communities and selling at local markets. Peter Brears records in his book *The English Country Potter* that at the beginning of the century there were over a hundred (at the end of the Second World War there were less than a dozen).

At art schools, students might take courses in the 'decorative' or 'applied' arts which would fit

them for their rôle in the industry, but they would be most unlikely to make pots themselves. Pottery departments were few and only slowly evolving: for example, it was not until 1926 that pottery came to be taught fully, under Dora Billington, at the Central School of Arts and Crafts in London.

The influence of Bernard Leach (1887–1979) – an artist who established a workshop – cannot be overestimated. Returning from Japan in the 1920s he insisted that all processes in pot making, from preparing the clay to firing the kiln, must be carried out by himself and his apprentices. In his workshop he trained such distinguished potters as Michael Cardew, Norah Braden, Katherine Pleydell Bouverie in this philosophy, and produced domestic ware at reasonable prices and of high quality, as well as individual pieces which were exhibited in galleries. These combined the attention to detail of form, the fluency of brush-work and understanding of glazes of the eastern tradition with the robustness of the ware and some of the techniques of the pre-industrial country potter.

At about the same time William Staite Murray (1881–1962) was treading a new path through his large, vigorously thrown individual pots. In the 1920s they were exhibited alongside fine art works in other media, titled like them and at comparable prices, in the Lefevre Gallery in London. In 1925 he became head of the pottery school at the Royal College of Art.

(Left) *Stoneware vase by Lucie Rie.*

103

The influence of these two through example and teaching, and Leach through his writings, was paramount between the wars – Leach with his fusion of eastern standards with the English tradition, and Staite Murray with the idea that clay might be used as an expressive medium. But both were, of course, throwers. Hand-building was not seriously practised until much later.

Two potters who helped to alter prevailing attitudes to the validity and worth of hand-building were Helen Pincombe and Ruth Duckworth. Helen Pincombe recalls that in her student days at the Central School there were only enough wheels to allow each student to throw for half an hour in each session, and that the rest of the time would be spent in coiling. It was a way of using time until the main craft – throwing – could be practised. There was little to be learnt about hand-building from museums; then, as now, exhibits bore only date and provenance. She could find only one study of the technique of coiling – that of the pot makers of the Pueblo Indians – and based her own method on that (see p. 93).

In that part of her career, through the Second World War and post-war period, there were few studio potters, and the very few buyers would consider their products only if they were useful. The first time she saw work which was sculptural rather than purely practical – for her 'refreshingly different' – was in 1960 at the first of Ruth Duckworth's exhibitions at Henry Rothschild's gallery 'Primavera', then in London (see pp. 22 and 94).

Ruth Duckworth was born in Germany in 1919 and came to England in 1936. She studied first sculpture and later, after meeting Lucie Rie in 1956, ceramics. Her chosen medium now became fired clay. Her work, vigorous and broad in scope, ranges from diminutive, fragile pieces in porcelain to large, life-sized stoneware sculptures and murals. At the time of that first exhibition she was spending half her time producing thrown table-ware, and the other half producing individual pieces, including large coiled pots. In 1964 she went to Chicago to teach

and little of her work has been seen here since.

The influence of these two was timely – Helen Pincombe through the courses she ran for teachers for the Society for Education through Art ('teachers who could not see beyond little wormy things 3″–4″ high'), and Ruth Duckworth through bringing to her work her own sculptural insights and through her teaching at the Central School.

At the same time, two of the most influential potters of the post-war years – Lucie Rie and Hans Coper – were developing their own styles. As it happens, Lucie Rie's work was entirely thrown, and Hans Coper always used thrown forms even when building composite pots. But their influence, and the forms they evolved, went beyond technique.

Both came to England before the Second World War – Lucie Rie from Vienna in 1938, and Hans Coper from Germany in 1939. But it was not until 1946 that Lucie Rie could set up her studio, with Hans Coper as one of her assistants. For her it was a return to clay; for him it was the first encounter, but he quickly came to terms with the medium. They produced a sophisticated range of table-ware in matt black and shiny white glaze, nearer to the Bauhaus than to Leach, and for this they were placed in the company of designers rather than artists. Victor Margrie writes: 'The restrained black and white forms . . . were strikingly modern and represented the new design consciousness of post-war Britain.'*

While they shared common interests, enthusiasms and sources, each eventually made individual pieces in his own style. Rie's work was delicate, the shapes often squeezed and pushed into asymmetrical forms – flattened bottles, ovalled bowls, square-sided cylinders with wonderfully rich and unexpected surfaces and colours. The cultivated surfaces – products of the interaction between body slip and glazes during firing – and the gently articulated forms, simple but tough, were never forced: they have an ineffable harmony.

Lucie Rie (see Bibliography)

Coper's work, partly inspired by modern sculptors such as Brancusi and Giacometti, was more adventurous in form though always hollow and described by him as 'pots'. He was not interested in colour, and used matt black and creamy white slip glazes to create beautifully refined, sensually restrained surfaces, enhancing but secondary to the form. Thrown shapes would be joined together and re-formed in unpredictable ways; coils would be added and thrown to make a flange springing from the waist of a form or a flat rim poised horizontally over the neck. For a brief period in the mid 1960s he would sometimes add coils, then throw them up to heighten monumental vases. Among the families of pots are large, flat spade shapes surmounting and growing out of stems, thistle-shaped pots, round boulder-like bases from which grow mighty necks and outflung lips, and small, precise delicate forms with bases poised on their own clay plinths. In spirit, even in appearance, many of them recall the classical archaic world, Cycladic and Neolithic figures or the beautifully wrought tools of the Bronze Age; others, like small libation cups, suggest ritual. They resonate with the past, are very much part of our present but belong to no time precisely. They are images of a new kind.

The work of both Lucie Rie and Hans Coper spoke out strongly in the 1950s, an antidote to the rustic and oriental influence which had prevailed for several decades. Many prominent potters who became internationally known in the 1970s had been taught by one or other: of those illustrated in this book are two as different from them, and from each other, as Elizabeth Fritsch and Ewen Henderson — both hand-builders and themselves influential on a younger generation.

In the last ten or twenty years the revival of hand-building has been obvious and exciting. We cannot separate the causes because they have acted on each other: no doubt it began with the expansion of higher education. Expanding art schools began to encourage hand-building, a new generation of potters quickly

Bottle by Hans Coper, c. 25 cm high, c. 1965.

emerged who included hand-building in their repertoire of techniques – among them Dan Arbeid, Ian Auld, Gordon Baldwin and James Tower. Many of the best and most original potters, including these four, became teachers, often part-time. But their influence extended beyond their students to a wider audience. Having financial security they were able to continue to develop, and to make – and exhibit – the slowly formed, experimental, individual pieces to which they could bring the aesthetic considerations normally associated with 'fine art'.

New galleries, new societies, specialist magazines and conferences, the rise of collecting, the establishment of the Crafts Council – all have contributed. Indeed, they have contributed to the burgeoning interest in pottery as a whole: the 'country potter' too can partake of the benefits offered. We can now see a new breed of country potter, often trained at art school, still able to set individuality and local connection against the power of industry: most towns and villages have them.

By now hardly any schoolboy or schoolgirl can be unaware of pottery: most will probably

Burnished black vessel in the form of a zebu. Gilan, ancient Iran, 1200–1000 B.C.

have experience of it. Very many schools are equipped with kilns and have specialist teachers: some of their pupils achieve very high standards in both throwing and hand-building.

Of course the affluence of the 1960s and 1970s accelerated these changes. But even now, in a world of contracting opportunity, the beginner is still able to take advantage of them. There is lively action, ready technical information, the possibility of well-equipped studios and of teaching by practising potters. He can see the work of the past and present well displayed in museums, and read about it in an extensive literature. He can be aware of the great freedom shown by potters in other countries – especially the USA. He need not feel that he is aiming for an artistic backwater: if he is an artist he can be an artist in pottery in a world where old barriers – between fine art and craft, or between one medium and another – are doomed to fade.

We are too close in time to this surge of interest in pottery to predict the future; we can only speak in the present, as we see and feel. In the end, aesthetic progress or change in any creative area arises either from individuals of immense originality and creativity or through technical discovery or advance. Surely the first is the

more important. Throughout the history of ceramics there have been unknown innovators who have re-routed traditional paths. But as we have seen, innovation in form and style can also exist within a tradition: Maria Martinez and Lesse Nampeyo are two who gave new thrust and life to traditional forms. And what of the spirit which lay behind the wonderful sculptural animal made between 1200 and 1000 B.C. in Gilan in ancient Iran? In two regions, Gilan and Luristan, the range and skill of the metal workers is notable, but only in Gilan is there a remarkable flair for pottery. How did this form arise, what was the creative drive which initiated it, was it an individual fulfilling a collective need by giving shape to a new reality?

But technical advance is important too: we may instance the impetus given to potters to produce delicate and refined objets when porcelain clay was marketed in the 1960s.

As individuals our creative progress will be marked by incidents of conceptual insight and of technical breakthrough. The tension which lies between content and technique is one which can be resolved only in the doing. While skills are not an end in themselves it is only by having them that one can be ready to recognise, and embody, those elusive hints of poetry, sensed fleetingly. They are hard enough to capture; most artists share a feeling that the thing they have imagined is bigger and more powerful than the object they succeed in making. Lucie Rie, though she revels in the unpredictability of the fire, still partly feels that what goes into the kiln is better than what comes out. Flaubert must have felt the same when he said of his craft: 'Human language is like a cracked kettle on which we beat out tunes for bears to dance to when all the time we are longing to move the stars with our pity'.

Most things we make are dependent on imagination for their making and for their enjoyment. Perhaps we may count ourselves lucky if our imagination outruns our skill, for while we must secretly acknowledge that ideal excellence is unattainable, we also *know* that the next image will be the best.

Notes on working with clay

The fact that beautiful pots can be built by hand in the most primitive as well as the most sophisticated circumstances may well have persuaded some readers who have not already done so to 'have a go' themselves. This book has not, of course, attempted to be a primer in hand-building, but there have been references to clay in its various states, and descriptions of processes in which it has been indicated that the clay has to be in a particular state at each stage. It may be useful to summarise in this 'footnote', in a more systematic way, the relevant characteristics of clay as a material, and to add a few points of practical guidance to help the beginner to approach his material with confidence.

Clay and its states

The nature of clay changes with its moisture content; it rarely remains static because in air it will always tend to dry. It can be watery enough to be more or less liquid, thin or thick: then it is called a 'slip'. The starting-point for most work, however, is clay in its plastic state, when it is damp but not sticky, and dry and firm enough to allow manipulating and modelling.

As it loses more moisture and becomes 'leather-hard' it will feel solid and firm but it will still be possible to move, beat, cut or carve it, or to add to it; it is at this stage that final shaping and decorating are usually carried out.

As the clay dries even more it begins to become brittle, to change colour and shrink. It can no longer be manipulated or added to, and decoration cannot be applied. Pots at this stage are known as 'green ware', but even now the clay can still be broken down in water and reconstituted.

Once the clay has been fired above 600°C, it has completely changed its nature: it has shrunk further but will now hold its shape in water and cannot be reconstituted; it has 'vitrified' and arrived at a state of permanence. At this stage it would be called 'biscuit' ware. It can be decorated by painting or 'resist' techniques. Or glaze can be applied and will be absorbed into the surface. After firing to the higher temperature at which a glaze vitrifies, or 'melts', a quite new surface results. To achieve particular decorative effects the pot – either biscuit or glazed – can be treated in various ways and fired repeatedly.

Practical considerations

We have been mainly concerned in this book with the building of forms by coiling and modelling. So we have to know how the state of the clay affects, first, the ease with which a coil can be added, and secondly, how it affects the processes of modelling.

The first question is easily answered: plastic clay sticks to plastic clay, so it is unnecessary to add water if two plastic surfaces are to be joined; a firm and reasonably large contact will suffice. But if plastic clay is to be joined to leather-hard clay, the hard surface must be scored and dampened with water at the point of contact. If leather-hard clay is to be joined to leather-hard clay, both surfaces must be scored and dampened. Clay is never joined to a bone-dry surface.

To answer the second question we remember that during drying the clay changes progressively from being plastic to being harder, stronger, but less malleable. In forming the pot the guiding principle is to have the clay at the working edge moist and plastic enough to allow joining, shaping and modelling, but dry enough away from the edge to be able to take the weight of any added clay. It is, of course, a gradual transition; the whole form must be flexible enough to respond to the shaping of the new coil. If, indeed, the form is complex, with abrupt changes in direction, it may have to be built in several stages.

We must remember too that clay shrinks as it dries. Thin walls dry more quickly than thick walls, so if they are part of the same form, drying must be very slow to avoid cracking.

If the pot is to be shaped after the form has been built, the state of the clay is crucial. Many potters shape from the *inside* of the pot, using a kidney-shaped metal or rubber scraper (or 'kidney scraper'). The wall is pressed out and up against the supporting and shaping hand on the outside, at the stage when the clay is fairly soft and pliable. If the form is to be shaped by beating, the clay must be allowed to harden a little. Scraping to remove bumps, to even the surface or to produce a texture is carried out when the clay is slightly drier still.

But how can we control – or slow down – the drying of the clay to meet these requirements? Essentially all we have to do is to keep it in a moist atmosphere, away from dry air or heat. This is set out below in more practical terms.

If you are waiting for the pot to dry to increase its strength for further work, keep the rim moist by wrapping a paper towel around it and dampening this with a sponge, or by loosely draping thin polythene sheeting over the form but in contact with the rim. If the rim has become rather drier than the clay to be added to it, score it with a pin tool, fork or wooden modelling tool and dampen it gently with a sponge. The scoring and the water provide a slip to which the new coil will adhere.

If the whole form has become too dry, drape a damp towel around it and cover it with polythene sheet, or bandage it with paper towelling and moisten the paper. Avoid getting water around or in the base, and keep an eye on it so that it does not become too wet and collapse.

Wrap the pot being built in polythene if you have to leave it for a while. Wrap any spare clay in polythene. If several coils have been rolled out at the same time, keep them loosely wrapped in polythene.

Always work on an absorbent surface – a wooden table or board – when you are kneading, wedging, or rolling out. The clay will dry a little but not stick. If it is already of the right consistency, sparingly dampen the working surface to prevent drying.

Build on an absorbent surface; the clay at the base will dry quickly without sticking and can then shrink without cracking. A small square of wood is best as this allows the pot to be moved about freely.

If the base is to be formed in a mould other than one of clay or plaster (both absorbent), line it first with a thin cloth, such as butter muslin, or paper, or a scattering of sand, so that the clay does not stick (ethnic potters use ash or dry dung). Pots beaten out on an inverted form must also be protected in the same way.

Remember that very dry clay is brittle and breaks easily, forming a very fine dust. So always wipe workbench and surfaces, tools and floor with damp cloths after each work session. If it is necessary to scrape a pot when it is dry, wear a face mask.

To go back to very first principles, make sure that you have got rid of air bubbles in the clay you use, and that you do not introduce any during forming. They will expand when the pot is fired and crack or shatter it! It is at the opening of the kiln that the proper handling of the clay at every stage will be rewarded. However experienced the potter this continues to be a moment of excited anticipation. Indeed, the whole route to the finished pot, from beginning to end, can be exciting, and is always involving. Even beginners, once they have confidence in the use of the material, can feel free to use imagination, intuition, and sense of rightness.

Mallam Garba smoothing the rim before shaping it.

Bibliography

Prehistoric and historic

Jōman Pottery J. Edward Kidder (Kodansha International 1968)

The Heritage of Japanese Ceramics Fijio Koyama translated by J. Figgess (Weatherhill 1973)

The Chinese Potter Margaret Medley (Cornell University Press 1976)

Life and Death of the Bronze Age Sir Cyril Fox (Routledge Kegan Paul 1959)

Ancient Iran P. R. S. Moorey (Ashmolean Publications 1975)

Ancient Cyprus A. C. Brown and H. W. Catling (Ashmolean Publications 1975)

Arthur Evans and the Palace of Minos Ann Brown (Ashmolean Publications 1983)

Pottery from the Nile Valley before the Arab Conquest Janine Bourniau (Fitzwilliam Museum, Cambridge University Press 1981)

Cypriot Art in the British Museum ed. B. F. Cook (British Museum Publications 1979)

'The Medieval Pottery Industry and Markets' S. A. Moorhouse, from *Medieval Industry*, ed. D. W. Crossley (C.B.A. Research Report no. 40, 1981)

David A. Hinton *Medieval Pottery of the Oxford Region* (Ashmolean Museum)

A History of Pottery Emmanuel Cooper (Longman 1972)

Icon and Idea Herbert Read (Faber & Faber 1955)

Contemporary Ethnic

The Traditional Pottery of Papua New Guinea Patricia May and Margaret Tuckson (Bay Books Publishing Co. 1983)

Nigerian Pottery Sylvia Leigh-Ross (Ibadan University Press for the Department of Antiquities, Lagos 1970)

Pioneer Pottery Michael Cardew (Longman 1979)

National Geographic, 162 1982 (on Pueblo Indians)

The Naked Clay (Museum of the American Indian 1972)

'The Potters of Thrapsano' Maria Voyatzoglou (*Ceramic Review*, no 24, 1973)

Contemporary

Primitive Pottery Hal Riegger (Van Nostrand Reinhold 1967)

The Potter's Challenge Bernard Leach (Souvenir Press 1976)

The English Country Potter Peter C. D. Brears (David and Charles 1971)

Hand-building Ceramic Forms Elsbeth S. Woody (John Murray 1979)

Hands in Clay – an introduction to ceramics Charlotte F. Speight (Alfred Publishing Co. 1979)

The Craft of the Potter Michael Casson (BBC Publications 1977)

Gordon Baldwin – a retrospective view (catalogue, Cleveland County Museum)

Lucie Rie ed. John Houston (Crafts Council Publications 1981)

Artist Potters in England Muriel Rose (Faber and Faber 1955)

Pottery in Britain Today Michael Casson (Alec Tiranti 1967)

Technical

The Potter's Dictionary of Materials and Techniques Frank Hamer (Pitman* 1975)

Ceramics for the Archaeologist Anna O. Shepard (Carnegie Institute of Washington 1956)

The journals *Ceramic Review* (ed. Eileen Lewenstein and Emmanuel Cooper, address, 21 Carnaby St, London W1V 1PH, pub. Craftsmen Potters Association of Great Britain) and *Crafts* (pub. Crafts Council) have been invaluable in providing leads and information.

*Now A & C Black.

Index